The Way It Was

Joe Quigley made his strike in the Kantishna. Fannie the Hike was a living legend even before they were married, in 1906.

The Way It Was

OF PEOPLE, PLACES AND THINGS IN PIONEER INTERIOR ALASKA

by

Jo Anne Wold

Drawings by Barbara Rinker Short

Alaska Northwest Publishing Company
Anchorage, Alaska

Library of Congress cataloging in publication data:

Wold, Jo Anne.
    The way it was: of people, places, and things in pioneer interior Alaska / by Jo Anne Wold; drawings by Barbara Rinker Short.
      p.   cm.
    ISBN 0-88240-316-8
    1. Frontier and pioneer life—Alaska—Fairbanks Region. 2. Fairbanks Region (Alaska)—Social life and customs. 3. Fairbanks Region (Alaska)—History. I. Title.
F914.F16W65 1988   88-3375
979.8 ′6—dc19   CIP

Designer: Shawn Lewis

Alaska Northwest Publishing Company
137 East Seventh Avenue
Anchorage, Alaska 99501

Printed in U.S.A.

CONTENTS

PREFACE

I have always been deeply curious about life in the North in the early days. What was it like? Who were the pioneers? Where did they come from? Why did they leave their homes and come here? What were their thoughts and hopes and dreams? I sought the answers and they became the accounts in this book, first written during the four years I was a columnist for the *Fairbanks Daily News-Miner*.

Fairbanks, where I have lived all my life, was the last of the big gold discoveries in the North. Pay dirt was struck here in 1901, four years after the Klondike discovery and two years after the Nome strike. Many of the miners who came here were graduates of the earlier gold-rushes, confident that they could get their share of the gold and get out.

But Fairbanks was a gold field with a difference: the gold was not for the sluicing, as it had been on the creeks of the Klondike and on the black-sand beaches of Nome. It was buried beneath frozen muck — hundreds of feet of the stubborn stuff — that had to be thawed to bedrock and dug out and hauled away.

Fairbanks was not an overnight success. That first year, when men in their tents and pitiful huts ate rabbit stew by the warmth of a Yukon stove, only forty thousand dollars in gold was recovered. It was clear that an infrastructure had to be built before mining could get a full head of steam.

Supplies had to come 2,700 miles by ocean vessel from Seattle to St. Michael, then 1,200 miles by sternwheeler up the Yukon and Tanana rivers, then be transferred to boats of shallower draft for the last lap, up the Chena. It was a six-week trip — if all went well, which often it did not. The Interior was at once harsh, inhospitable and painfully remote.

Those men and women tempered by the earlier stampedes, already tried by deprivation, made their way into the heart of the vast Interior with little more than instinct to guide them. Others came armed with only able bodies, a little vision and a lot of daring, into a country of which they were fatefully ignorant — a country notoriously unkind to strangers. All of them scaled mountains, crossed glaciers, shot rapids, forded icy streams, and those who survived to get here felled trees and built a town that would, within ten years, be the largest in the Territory.

They were not the gun-toting, booze-guzzling, high-rolling renegades and loose women who make sensational copy. They were hard-working men and women, most of them God-fearing and often teetotalling. Nor were they all miners. There were freighters and steamboat men, storekeepers and farmers, teachers and nurses, lawyers and laborers. There were men on the run, and women breaking loose from tradition. They came from the East Coast, the West Coast, the Deep South and the Midwest. They came from Australia, Japan, Russia, Scandinavia, Yugoslavia, the British Isles, Canada and places between. All were part of a society in turmoil, and all were seeking a better life.

Two years after its founding, Fairbanks was an incorporated city with a mayor, a council and a school. In short order it had telephone service, electric lights, a fire department, a narrow-gauge railroad, two newspapers, hotels with bay windows. There were striped awnings and plate-glass windows in the shopping district. There was an indoor swimming pool and a curling rink. There was the Bohemian Club, men only, where they wore tuxedoes and drank beer from imported German steins.

In spite of its amenities, Fairbanks streets were ankle-deep in mud, or dust; the sidewalks were rough-hewn boards; the primitive log cabins had crude outhouses in back, and in some neighborhoods the slop water was thrown into the street.

It was at heart a boom town. In 1904 there were thirty-three bars on Front Street, and they never closed. There was a red light district in the center of town, surrounded by a high picket fence to shield it from the eyes of the innocent — or give cover to the customers. Gambling was wide open, and a jail was one of the first public buildings to be erected.

And yet Attorney John Clark, who came to Fairbanks in 1906 and practiced law for a quarter of a century, remarked about the early years, "There were no gun fights, as I do not suppose one man in five hundred carried a gun. Fist fights were few, for while men would get drunk occasionally, they were not a quarrelsome lot, being young men who came here from a spirit of adventure. . . They gathered in the saloons and dance halls at night, as there was no other place to go."

To piece together a panorama of life as it was for those remarkable people, I read books about the gold camps, talked to pioneers and their descendants, discovered unpublished letters and manuscripts. Many of the accounts were written long after the experiences, as those early settlers had little time for record-keeping. Their concerns were about getting the basic necessities. Of their accomplishments, some of them quite incredible, they were matter-of-fact, as if their encounters with the vastness of Alaska had taught them humility.

Through it all they lived the rule of goodwill toward men. They stopped to help the fellow on the trail, they left wood in the cabin for the next traveler, they shared their bacon and beans.

The stories here fall into four sections. In "Lifestyles" we explore the pursuits of some stalwart men and women, new Alaskans of nearly a century ago, who sought a better life, dreamed new dreams, trod unknown paths in an unwelcoming land.

There are few monuments in the North, but there are landmarks. We examine some of these in "Landmarks." Remembrances of those who passed this way once-upon-a-time are of trails that have become highways, buildings now on the National Register of Historic Places, a long-gone roadhouse, a once-thriving brewery, a swinging bridge — now merely the stuff of nostalgia. By signposts such as these we trace our past, and we read the signs for deeper meaning.

As I read and wrote about the early settlers, memories of my own life came to mind. Having lived all my forty-seven years in Fairbanks, I too have joined the ranks of the pioneers and I have things to tell about "the way it was."

My father, Arnold Wold, a Norwegian from Duluth, Minnesota, was twenty-four when he came to Alaska in 1926 to join his older brother, Sig, in McCarthy, a town that came to life and thrived and died with the Kennecott Copper Company's nearby mine.

Uncle Sig, a vigorous and determined entrepreneur, had all bases covered in McCarthy. He owned a taxi service, a laundry, a hotel and a boarding house. He delivered water and ice and emptied the honey buckets — all with the same truck. Daddy worked for him until 1932, then came to Fairbanks and took a job as a mechanic for the Fairbanks Exploration Company.

On a trip back to Duluth in 1934, Daddy met Eleanor Helen Gatzek, a vivacious, hazel-eyed Polish girl of nineteen. Two years later Daddy proposed by mail, and in the spring of 1936 Mother came to Fairbanks and they were married. Home was a small cabin, no running water, with a wood stove and a "whozit," as Mother called the privy in the backyard. A year later my sister Kay was born, and I arrived the following April. Bonnie, the youngest of us, came in 1943.

"Scenes from Childhood" covers some of my memories of growing up in Fairbanks.

Under "Destinies" we follow, through accounts they left behind, four persons of widely divergent backgrounds and talents, from widely separated spots on the earth, whose pathways converged in the North. What they sought and what they found were as varied as their beginnings, and yet they shared in the taming of a frontier, the building of a new society. They are prototypes of those who link us with the past, as we link them to the future.

Lifestyles

THE TEN COMMANDMENTS

When the intrepid pioneers shouldered their backpacks and came into the little-known North, the laws were sketchy and the enforcers of those laws were few and far between. Government of our forefathers was not imposed from without, but from within.

Here are the Miners' Ten Commandments as Martin Harrais, gold-miner, railroad-builder and scholar, found them nearly ninety years ago, tacked to the wall of a cabin in Dawson:

Thou shalt have no other claim but one on any one creek.

Thou shalt not make unto the recorder any false statements concerning thy discovery or the labor by which thou holdest thy claim; for thy Uncle Sam is a jealous uncle, visiting thine iniquities upon thy head in case of contest, and showing mercy onto all such as keep his laws.

Thou shalt not take the name of the Lord thy God in vain when thou breakest thy windlass rope, for it doesn't do a damn bit of good.

Thou shalt not go prospecting again before thy claim givest out; neither shalt thou take thy gold dust to the gaming table; for monte, faro, roulette and poker will prove to thee that the more thou puttest down, the less thy takest up.

Thou shalt not remember what thy friend do at home on the Sabbath Day. Six days shalt thou dig or pick all that thy body can stand; but on the seventh thou shalt wash all thy dirty shirts, darn all thy socks, tape thy boots, make thy bread and boil thy pork and beans.

Thou shalt not grow discouraged, nor think of going home to thy father and thy mother until thou hast made thy stake.

Thou shalt not salt thy claim to sell it to a cheechako.

Thou shalt not commit assault and battery, unless thy neighbor jumps thy claim.

Thou shalt not bear false witness about "good paydirt in the creeks" to benefit a friend who has boats and provisions to sell.

Thou shalt not covet thy neighbor's cash, nor his tools; nor pick out nuggets from the company's pan and put them into thy mouth.

[Apropos the second commandment: when Harrais reached Dawson, 1897, many people assumed the Klondike was Uncle Sam's territory.] Granted the above may not be so reverent nor so poetically expressed as the original Ten Commandments, but as one miner said, "They sure packed a wallop!" Whenever a flagrant violation occurred, the men gathered, appointed a judge and a jury, and a miners' meeting was under way. In most cases the guilty were punished by banishment from the country. Imprisonment was not considered. It would only provide free room and board.

Martin Harrais recalled a time when two men were found guilty of robbing another man's cache. They were put on a log raft with three days' provisions and sent down the Yukon. "That put the fear of the Lord into other violators — if there were any," Harrais wrote, "and during my first year in Dawson I saw pans of gold left unattended in tents, and no one touched them."

The means of dealing with violators were harsh, swift and effective, but the most effective crime deterrent was the government within each man. Without crime, there is no need for punishment.

Episcopal Bishop Peter Trimble Rowe, who first came to Alaska in 1895, remarked on his forty-first trip into the country: "There is no other place where there is so little evil and wrongdoing . . . The average of clean manhood is higher throughout the Territory than Outside."

Rex Beach summed up the Code of the North in his book, *The Spoilers,* when he wrote, "You was in trouble — that's unfortunate; we help you — that's natural; no questions asked — that's Alaska."

Lifestyles

J.G. RIVERS

There is no excuse, in these days of tape recorders, for not taking down family history. We do not mean the dry stuff of genealogy, we mean the living history of what family members did, how they did it, what they thought, whom they met, and why their lives took certain turns. We want the down-to-earth, honest-to-God details. We want to live their lives with them.

How much richer we would be with insights into the hearts of those who went before us. Official records and newspaper stories have their place, but the most revealing are personal accounts from the trailblazers themselves, to tell us the way things were.

No doubt we all have regrets for stories we heard that are now forgotten. Some ideas are never recaptured once the immediate flush is gone, and we are left with fuzzy memories — not the stuff from which histories are written.

Fortunately for us, there was a Professor Cecil Robe in the University of Alaska history department forty years ago, who asked his students to write term papers recounting some aspect of family or regional history. These papers, preserved by Robe, who now lives in Eugene, Oregon, were recently donated to the University of Alaska Archives.

One paper was written by Fern Rivers, who recorded the events when her father, Julian Guy Rivers, came into the country more than seventy years ago. She said, "This story is meant to give a more intimate picture of Alaska as it used to be." It was written in 1941 from her father's viewpoint.

In the spring of 1906, in the hold of the old *Cottage City,* J.G. Rivers (whose son, Ralph, would some day be the first U.S. Congressman from Alaska) and three companions were bound for Skagway. They boarded as machinist's helpers and thus worked their way north in the hold, foregoing the beauties of the Inside Passage. J.G. had left a job with the Seattle Transfer Company where he had worked for eight years. As he put it, "With no further advancement in sight, and being by nature unfit for routine work, I decided to try Alaska." Rivers was twenty-five.

J.G. Rivers, attorney: "Life was a struggle, but I wonder where else a man trained as a bookkeeper could have done half so well."

It was late June when the party shouldered grub sacks and hiked White Pass en route to Whitehorse, where they arrived four days later, plagued by mosquito bites and with swollen, blistered feet. Here is J.G.'s account as Fern wrote it:

Here we secured a new flat-bottomed boat with oars, a pot of beans that would fill a five-gallon can, a few loaves of bread and some butter. Not a fancy menu, I grant you, but one of considerable substance and staying power.

All went well with our little ship and crew for the first few hours, and in fact until we hit Lake Lebarge. This is quite some lake of fifty-odd miles in length that kicks up quite a rumpus in a gale. We encountered rough weather when about halfway across the lake, and we were obliged to beach our craft in the lee of a small island. We waited twenty-four hours for calmer weather.

The rest of our trip downstream was delightful. We ran the boat, that is, allowed the current to carry us downstream at the leisurely speed of four or five miles an hour, putting into shore from time to time to warm our beans.

We reached Five Finger Rapids about midnight. I was at the oars and Sam was the captain. These rapids are quite swift, but safe enough if you know the right channel. Sam had been down them before so we were fortunate in that respect. When Sam was sure we were near the rapids he called to me, "There they are! Pull hard to the left and we'll hit 'em square." Buckley must have been sleeping with one eye open. He pulled the blanket over his head and said, "My God! What next!" After that Buckley couldn't turn around but some one would sing out, "My God! What next!"

The worst experience from here on to Dawson was when we discovered that our beans had gone sour and there was nothing left to eat. This happened a full day's journey from Dawson.

We found the capital of the Klondike all decked out in gala attire. Both American and Canadian flags were unfurled to the breeze. It was a joint celebration of Dominion Day and the Fourth of July, and some time it proved to be! We didn't feel like strangers in a strange land; we felt right at home. Everyone treated us fine, and no one cared where we came from.

. . . The people of that frontier camp were fine in every respect. They were generous to a fault, and not at all clannish or interested in your nationally. We were never socially prominent, but we had a host of friends.

J.G.'s wife, Flora, brought their two sons to Dawson after he was settled, but left their very small daughter with relatives in Seattle. Mrs. Rivers died soon afterward. J.G. never sent for the girl. He remained in the Dawson area for six years, during which he was employed by the Yukon Gold Company, a branch of the Guggenheim Company. "It was my ambition to learn all I could of modern mining methods," he said.

One spring Rivers was chosen by the company to help move the Number 7 dredge from Dawson to Iditarod. The completed dredge, nearly a thousand tons, was loaded on barges and towed by the steamer *Susie*. To quote again:

> This trip was without event as we floated down the Yukon, stopping at Eagle for customs clearance and proceeding to Holy Cross, near the mouth of the Iditarod River. Here we left the *Susie* and the barges were put in charge of smaller steamers for the long, tedious upstream push on the Iditarod.
>
> The low stage of water at the time made it impossible to push these heavily laden barges farther upstream, so I was left to sort out the material first needed in the construction of the dredge and have it relocated on horse scows and sent on.
>
> The horse scows are light-draft when loaded with twenty or twenty-five tons, and draw from ten to twelve inches of water. On the forward deck of the scow there is a platform on which the horse stands when riding, and there is a pusher gas engine to push the scow on the deep stretches of the river.
>
> The horse is trained to jump off when the barge approaches shallow water, tighten up on the tow cable, and help the loaded barge over the riffles. Once again approaching deep water, the horse jumps back on the platform and waits for his next stunt.

During the ten years Rivers was in Flat he worked for various mining companies, married Mae Cahill "a very charming and popular young lady," and took up the study of law. He was admitted to the bar in Flat in 1922. He and Mae had five children. When they moved to Fairbanks, Rivers established a law office on Second Avenue. They made their home in a log cabin a few blocks from the center of town.

After living in the North nearly forty years, Rivers said, "When I think of my life in Alaska with so little in the way of worldly wealth to show for it; of the struggle we have had in raising and educating our children; and the privations my wife has been obliged to suffer to take care of the children — I wonder whether it has all been worth-while. On the other hand, I often wonder whether there is a place on God's earth where a man, trained as a common bookkeeper, could have done half so well."

W.A. COGHILL

A nother of those hardy souls who came to the North with strength, stamina and a great desire to succeed, but zero dollars in their pockets, was W.A. Coghill. From Shrewsbury, England, of Scottish parentage, he broke away from the Old Country at twenty-three, after serving seven years as an apprentice to a printer and two more in the Typographical Union in Liverpool and South Wales.

In Seattle he became acquainted with two lumbermen. All three booked passage for Valdez in the spring of 1908, and walked the Valdez Trail to Fairbanks.

"There was still much snow on the trail when we started out," Coghill told his oldest son, William, who recorded his father's experiences for a history class at the University of Alaska in 1940. "At some points, especially going over Thompson Pass, the snow was so deep it almost completely buried the roadhouses. Some nights we would stop at a roadhouse, but usually we made camp and cooked our own meals. The trip, taking about ten days, was long, tiresome and tedious, yet very interesting.

"After we found a cabin the first thing we set about doing was getting a bath and washing our clothes. This had to be repeated night and morning for several days to rid ourselves of the unwelcome company of lice we picked up on the route."

Coghill's first job was at Goldstream, running a wheelbarrow in a drift mine ten hours a day for five dollars, plus room and board, but that was not what he had come to Alaska for. After two days he was ready to quit. The foreman encouraged him to wait since he was the only man on the job who could speak English, but he did not stay long.

He landed a job in his trade — setting type at the *Fairbanks Times*. Later W.F. Thompson, a reporter and printer, asked Coghill to help him produce a newspaper at Ridge Top during the campaign of Judge James Wickersham, who was then running for Alaska Representative.

W.A. Coghill, apprentice printer from England to prosperous Nenana businessman, tended bar in Fairbanks as a stopgap.

After the election Thompson continued the paper from the town of Chena, under the banner *Tanana Mines*. It came out weekly during the winter of 1908-1909. At that time Chena was quite a lively place, having two general stores, a saloon, a restaurant, a lumber yard, a fire department and chief of police.

"In the spring of 1909 Thompson started the *News Miner* in Fairbanks," Coghill said. "I asked Thompson for a job circulating his paper to the creeks and he made me a proposition: he would give me the papers for the first month and thereafter I was to pay five cents a copy. My circulation area spread to Ester." The competing paper was the *Fairbanks Morning Times*.

"That first month I carried my papers, making the trip both ways on foot, which meant plenty of walking as I had to deliver one hundred papers. My receipts from that first month amounted to more than four hundred dollars which I used to buy a horse and a two-wheeled cart. Being spring, the road was in deplorable condition. The wheels of the cart sank so deep that the bottom of the cart would drag in the mud."

While delivering the evening paper, Coghill became well acquainted with the Ester miners and so it was natural for them to ask, "Coggie, when you are in town will you pick some things up for me?" Thus his paper delivery expanded into an express business. Coghill received from ten to thirty-three percent commission on all items purchased from the stores in Fairbanks.

From a horse and cart Coghill graduated to a new car — a one-cylinder Brush — which he outfitted with a carrier. He was able to make two trips a day, carrying freight as well as passengers. Many a miner trusted his cleanup to Coghill, who rode with his feet on the pokes of gold all the way to the bank.

If a side of beef was tied on the running board, the passengers would have to climb through the window, but in those days people took such things in stride. Sometimes when the Brush one-cylinder was heavily loaded, the passengers would get out and push the car over the hill. At that time no one had to carry a license for either car or driver.

In 1916 Coghill sold out his Fairbanks interests and moved to Nenana, where he bought a combination hotel, restaurant, and merchandise business. He recognized that Nenana — which was just a camp at the time — would have a prosperous future when the proposed Alaska Railroad was built. The town became the head-quarters for the Alaska Railroad Construction Company, and employed a great many men. Everyone was making money, business boomed, and the town flourished. There were telephone service, a telegraph station, fire department, daily newspaper, movie house, public school, hospital, three churches, several restaurants and pool halls. The railroad accounting office was there, the commissary, machine shop, and roundhouses. The power plant supplied both electrical energy and steam heat for the town.

In the spring of 1919 Coghill made a trip back to England. He had been away twelve years. He left Nenana on the railroad as far as Healy, then by dog team to Talkeetna. "We traveled through the canyon along the frozen river, and how we ever made it is a mystery to me," he said.

In Talkeetna Coghill boarded the train again and rode in comfort to Seward, where he took a steamship to the West Coast. A month later he was in England.

In Neath, South Wales, a girl waited for him. Their courtship by mail was over. They were married and promptly sailed for New York. Their honeymoon of two months took them to Seattle, Skagway, Dawson and ever so leisurely down the Yukon and eventually to Nenana.

Business was at its peak during the 1920s while the railroad was under construction. The building of the huge steel bridge over the Tanana River was the final step. Coghill said, "I was aboard the first passenger train to travel over the bridge. I was also present at the ceremony in Nenana on July 15, 1923, when President Harding drove the golden spike marking the completion of the Alaska Railroad."

Descendants of W.A. Coghill are still in business in Nenana.

EDWARD H. STROECKER

It is possible, it seems to me, to look back and see how a man's life is directed into the thing he was meant to do.

Let us consider the case of Edward H. Stroecker. He traveled many a weary mile, taking on many a tiresome job and nearly settling for the humdrum life as a store accountant. He later became president of the First National Bank of Fairbanks.

It happened like this, according to a history paper that Ed's son, Bill, wrote when he was in college: In 1898, when news of the great Klondike gold rush stirred the spirit of thousands of adventurers in the States, Stroecker was twenty-one, working quietly in an accounting office in San Francisco. As he was not the type to rush into things, it was a year and a half later when Ed set out for the gold fields of Alaska. He was persuaded, in part, to go on this adventure by his mother, who thought he would appreciate home more on his return.

In April, 1900, Ed and eleven companions sailed out of the Golden Gate on board the schooner *Mary Sachs,* a sixty-two-foot windjammer. Actually, the word "sailed" is misleading. The boat, operated by a motley crew, nearly went down in a sixty-mile gale but, despite such setbacks, what will be will be, and the vessel reached Dutch Harbor twenty-five days later.

Pushing along Bristol Bay, the *Mary Sachs* docked at the mouth of the Kuskokwim River, where Stroecker and three other men rowed a small boat up the river with mining on their minds. They found no gold, but they took the job as U.S. census-taker, counting the Indian population. It paid four dollars a day.

That summer Stroecker and his mates paddled 650 miles up the Kuskokwim. They came back down the river in September to rendezvous with the *Mary Sachs* for the return trip to San Fran-

Edward H. Stroecker, not destined to make it big in gold-mining, took any available job on his way to becoming president of a bank.

cisco. Ed had been away from home six months. A month later he turned down an accounting job on a sugar plantation in Hawaii to head back to Alaska.

This time Stroecker went to Valdez accompanied by his friend, Oscar Hultburg. It was the dead of winter when they landed. They waited two months before setting out for a mining venture on Slate Creek with their provisions and a team of four dogs. The Valdez Glacier had to be crossed in a storm, but, God willing, they made it. Ed and Oscar mined most of the summer then returned to Valdez, where Stroecker took a job as bartender at the Montana Saloon.

Valdez in those days had a population of nearly one thousand and as in all boom towns, life there was spirited, to say the least. Fort Liscum, four miles across the bay, sent a steady stream of soldiers into town all winter. There were also many government packers building a telegraph line from Valdez to Eagle. The breweries, the saloons, the hotels and cafes, even the churches and schools were not in want for patrons. The following spring Stroecker was back on the creeks again, but prospecting was not good. That winter he tended bar again.

For two more years Stroecker tried his luck at mining, but without much success. In the fall of 1904 he and three other men were mining near Chisana, one of the sources of the Tanana, when they decided to whipsaw lumber, build a boat, and go down the Tanana to Fairbanks, the scene of the Pedro gold strike. It was late in the fall, freezing weather, and the Indians advised the miners not to go. They went anyway, and after capsizing, losing their bedding, a bag of flour, and their caribou meat, they sighted Fairbanks on October 4.

After living in a tent on the banks of the Chena for several days, Stroecker and his companions built a cabin. Jobs were scarce. Stroecker dug the foundation for the California Saloon (later the Chena Bar). "That time of year it was hard digging," Stroecker said. "But I was up against it and took any job available."

Their first winter in Fairbanks Stroecker went to Cleary Creek and worked for "Swiftwater" Bill Gates on Discovery Bench. Somehow he was destined not to make it big in gold mining — but he kept trying. In the spring of 1905 he stampeded to Kantishna, but returned to Fairbanks a month later. He took on a variety of jobs — ax-man for the Murphy Ditch survey crew, a woodcutter, a packer for the Alaska Road Commission, and mail carrier to Fort Gibbon.

In August of 1906 he and two partners established a wood camp five miles from Fairbanks where, working with a crew of nine men, they cut two thousand cords of wood for the Northern Commercial Company boilers supplying steam heat and electricity for Fairbanks. Perhaps it was the effects of an injured knee and a strained back that turned Stroecker once again to accounting. He became bookkeeper, credit man and collector for E.R. Peoples, a general merchandise house. He worked there eleven years, with one last and disappointing stampede to the Kuskokwim until Peoples sold out to the N.C. Company.

Stroecker then went to work as teller at the First National Bank, which is still in its original location at Second and Cushman. Six months later he was cashier. In ten years, 1929, Stroecker became president, a position he held until his death in 1952.

Is there now a pattern in all this? Was Stroecker thwarted in his mining ventures so he would find the door of the bank open to him? When Stroecker was interviewed on the KFAR radio program, "Here's A Pioneer," he said, "I get a great deal of pleasure in going over things that happened in the past." Did he consider the pattern of his life, and those things which are meant to be?

CATHERINE AND AARON VAN CURLER

Catherine and Aaron Van Curler were part of the great tidal wave of people who swept onto the shores of Lynn Canal in 1898. It was August when they landed at Skagway. A year later they were in Dawson, living in a crude cabin with windows made of empty beer bottles and caulked with moss. After working a lay on Bonanza and Hunker creeks for four years, the Van Curlers took a steamer to Fairbanks.

There they built a cabin in the wilderness town which was in the throes of a two-year-old gold stampede. In 1907 the Van Curlers staked ground 160 miles up the Chena River, with the idea of mining the riverbed. Before they could begin mining they had to cut a trail to the property, carry in supplies, build a cabin, and erect a six-hundred-foot dam across the Chena to divert the water. For such a monumental task they needed hand tools, strength of body and an enormous amount of endurance.

In a simple, handwritten account Catherine Van Curler tells of their humble beginning:

We cut our own trail up the Chena River. With three dogs and a small outfit we camped wherever night overtook us. The next summer we took 1,900 pounds of supplies upriver in a poling boat. It took us thirty days to make one hundred sixty miles by water, the worst water ever poled upstream by any woman and man. It was almost one continuous riffle.

We landed at our mine October 1, 1907, where the real work began — to build a cabin without horse or nails. Husband cut the logs and poles to cover the roof. We hauled them on skids to the boat, and then poled them to where we built our first real home in Alaska. I peeled the logs on one side, and we put them up as far as we could put them. We pulled them up by arm power. In ten days we had a cozy three-room cabin made.

In the spring we cut timber to put in a dam six hundred feet long across the Chena. Then our troubles began. First we had to make a new channel to divert the water. We cut moss and muskeg by the days and weeks. Then we took our pick and shovel to dig the new riverbed. Oh, the weary hours we spent to cut that new channel. No one knows but ourselves. We worked from twelve to twenty hours a day. In three years we had the new channel cut through, and we were drying out one-half mile of the main river.

Husband and I whipsawed enough lumber to make forty-eight boxes and fourteen flume boxes. We set them up in the bed of the river, and started to shovel in. One month a big rain came and raised the river until our new channel could not take all the water. So it tore out eighty feet of our dam, and took a lot of our tools. We saved the boxes and flumes which were tied together with cables and ropes.

We started to work on the new channel to widen it and make it deeper. That took months. Then we started to replace the broken part of our dam. We had to travel upriver one-half mile to cut timber. Husband and I packed it one thousand feet on our shoulders to the river, where we floated it to the dam site. After landing all the timber we needed, we cut acres and acres of moss for the toe pilings. We carried all the moss in a wheelbarrow with him on the front end and me on the back. We packed moss until two o'clock in the morning, and then went home to rest, get a cup of coffee, and do the same thing over again.

When we had enough moss, we started to close up the break. We worked all day and up to three o'clock in the morning. Then we went out in the boat and hauled in tons and tons of rock to put on the moss in front of the pilings. Oh, the weary hours we put in early and late. But we got it done in ten days. At last we could sluice again. We sluiced until freeze-up.

The next spring, after we thought the danger was passed, the dam went out again. With many days of hard work and sleepless nights of carrying timber and moss, we repaired the dam again. It went out three times that summer. Each time we repaired it, the job got a little harder. We only sluiced ten days that season.

The next year we were ready for a good season. Husband and I got the summer wood hauled and sawed up. A couple of young fellows came along so we hired them for the summer. We got to sluicing early, and everything was going along so nice. I had killed a moose in front of the house, and we were rejoicing at my good fortune.

As the days went along, the weather did not look very good. One night when it was quite cloudy I said to my husband and the two boys, "Hadn't we better clean up the boxes in case it rains and causes the river to rise and the dam to break!"

"Oh, no," Van said, "we have the boxes well tied, and I don't look for the water to rise much. I believe the dam will hold."

But, oh, at three o'clock in the morning I heard an awful racket. I jumped out of bed and saw our dam gliding along downstream. I called Van and the boys. They came running out just in time to see our forty-eight sluice boxes and sixteen flume boxes going downstream. It was a sorrowful thing to see so much hard labor lost.

The next day when the water had gone down, we went to look for the shovels, picks, pans and other tools. Almost everything was gone. We found one sluice box turned upside down. We turned it over, and took the riffle out. We got one ounce of gold. We went a little farther downriver and found another sluice box with one-half ounce of gold. That was all we had to buy our winter grubstake. Van was terribly discouraged. We let the two boys go, and gave them twenty dollars until we could pay them up.

Well, we decided we would put the dam in again. One hundred feet had gone out, but we started with a stout heart, and lots of willpower. We began by cutting timber and carrying it out on our shoulders to the river. Run it down the river to the dam. Cut moss and fill in the break. It was freeze-up before we got it finished. Then it was time to get our winter meat. After that we started cutting logs so we could make sluice boxes in the spring. With our five faithful dogs we hauled the logs one and a half miles.

Catherine and Aaron Van Curler tried to divert the Chena and mine the riverbed. The elements doomed them to failure.

By December we had cut and hauled forty-eight logs. After that it was time for Van to make three trips to Fairbanks to haul our supplies so we could save ten cents a pound in freight. I stayed alone while he made the trips. He was gone fifteen to twenty days each trip. Not a person did I see all those days. From 1910 until 1917 I stayed home every winter, and in the summer I helped my husband shovel dirt into the sluice boxes each day. By then we got our dam to hold.

During our hard luck and hard work, we both enjoyed the life we lived. After seven years we decided to spend the winters in Fairbanks. In the fall we closed the cabin and walked eighty miles to town with the three dogs pulling the sled with the camp outfit and five days' worth of grub. That was before there were any roadhouses. We would pitch a tent, or if we were too tired, we just spread our robe on the spruce boughs — with the snow up to our knees — and slept under the stars. We got up at daylight, and hit the trail after a light breakfast. I have walked that eighty miles five times. One trip coming to town I had thirty pounds on my back, and Van had forty-five pounds. All of our dogs had died but one, so that meant we walked.

In the spring we went back out to our mine by boat with our eighteen hundred pounds of supplies. Van and I poled that one hundred and sixty miles over the roughest water that ever ran downstream. It took us fifteen to twenty days to land it. We made four trips by boat. The river was not safe; there were new channels every year, so we quit poling upriver.

We bought a horse, and freighted with him three years. The third year the horse fell over a steep bank, landed on some logs, and broke his back. That meant we had to freight with dogs another few years. Later we bought another horse, and one spring I made a trip alone with the faithful old animal. I started from Fairbanks with eighteen hundred pounds on a double-ender. The horse was so tall I had to take a block of wood to stand on to harness him. It snowed and blowed. We got into a lot of deep snowdrifts. It was a little hard shoveling the horse out of the deep snow.

I enjoyed every minute of my long trip alone. I had a rooster in a box and he kept me company, as he would crow and crow as soon as he saw daylight. I was on the trail five days. The snow filled the road with drifts four feet high, but I got home without any trouble.

In the spring of 1930 we hired a freighter to take our outfit to the mine. His team played out forty-five miles from home. We were stranded on a muskeg flat with twenty-eight hundred pounds of grub and tools. There was no timber to build a cache, so we put a tent over our supplies and tied it down good.

Van put as much freight as our three dogs could haul on a hand sled, and we started for home. By then the snow was melting fast, so we had to travel at night when the trail was firmer. We made it home in three days.

After the ice went out in the Chena, Van loaded our scow with three dogs and a toboggan, and we started downriver eighty miles. The first thing we had to do was build a road one and a half miles so we could move our cache to the river.

Van and I took an ax and cut eight-foot-long timber as big as a stovepipe. We had to pack the timbers to the road site. That took two and a half days. Then we placed the timbers across the muskeg a foot apart. On the third day we started with the toboggan to haul the outfit to the river.

By that time a bear had gotten into our grub and destroyed four hundred pounds. The dogs smelled the bear and ran away, but they came back. We put two hundred pounds on the toboggan and started for the river. We hauled three loads a day. It took us four days to haul it to the river. When we were finished, Van shot the bear. It was a big black one.

On the fifth day we loaded the boat with nineteen hundred pounds, and built a high cache to store the balance of the outfit. On the ninth day we started home poling upriver in our scow. Oh, man, then our troubles began. It took eight days of hard poling and wading to go fifteen miles. We unloaded two hundred and fifty pounds and cached it in a cabin.

We started again. Now maybe you don't think we had a rough time. The riffles were so steep we worked five hours to get over one riffle. We worked from five o'clock in the morning until eleven o'clock at night. We pulled the boat to the bank, and rolled up in our blanket any place we could find dry timber for a fire. We were so worn out, cold and wet. Of course, that was all in a day's work.

We had a two-hundred-fifty-foot boat line. Sometimes Van would be pulling and I leading the scow, and sometimes I would take the line and go ahead, and Van would lead the scow. When we came to a bad riffle, one of us would go the length of the line and tie it to a tree as far ahead as it would reach. Then hand-over-hand we would pull the scow up to where the rope was tied. The next bad piece of water we came to, we would do the same thing over again.

We poled and tied lines until we were all in. Laid up one day for rest. We saw bear, moose, beaver, mink, otter and caribou. When we were halfway home, we stopped again at a relay station. Van built a windlass and fastened it to the bow of the scow with the two hundred and fifty feet of rope. When we got to a bad riffle we would windlass ourselves over it. Oh, it was such a big help to us in getting the scow up.

We got within twenty-five miles of home where we cached all our grub in a cabin. We rested four days before we started walking home. I had butter and bacon. Van had flour. We put canned stuff on the dogs' backs. We had a long, hard trail of muskegs to cross. Anyone who has traveled over them knows what a rough time it is. We thought the mosquitoes would eat us up before we got home, all wore out. We were gone almost a month. That was our last river work.

In 1933 we came to Fairbanks. Van's health gave out due to hard work and hardships. In 1935 I had the misfortune of getting mixed up with a truck. I broke my leg in three places and badly hurt my foot. I was in the hospital ten months where everyone was kind to me. Thanks to the doctors and nurses. So ended our long usefulness to Alaska as pioneers. We feel proud that we are pioneers. No one can take this memory from us of being a man and wife helping to make Alaska.

HARD-LUCK POZZA

W hen Klondike gold was struck in 1896, Austrian-born Emil Pozza was twenty-six and in Manitoba, Canada, working for a wealthy man who offered to outfit him and three other men — John Piska, George Renard and Jack Greer — to seek their fortune in Dawson. That was an offer Pozza could not refuse.

The party took the railroad to Vancouver, British Columbia, and made their way by boat to Juneau. It was then mid-May, 1897. A steamer took Pozza and his companions to Dyea, where they gathered their goods and mounted the Chilkoot. "Believe me, there was no fun," Emil wrote in his memoirs:

> At Lake Bennett there was a sawmill from which we bought lumber and my partner built a boat twenty-six feet long and six feet wide. We got a sail and with our outfit in the boat started going toward the gold discovery. Lake Bennett is about twenty miles long, and narrow. Hills on both sides of the lake make the winds strong.

Hard-Luck Emil Pozza failed to alter his destiny by hard work.

Old Man Piska, as we called him since he was forty-five and head of the party, was steering the boat and he kept shouting to us to put down the sail, but we were so frightened we couldn't move. Finally we landed at Lake Tagish. We were surprised that we didn't drown. I think the twenty miles were made in about forty-five minutes.

When we got to the head of Whitehorse Rapids we stopped on the left side and took a good look at the rapids. They didn't look very good to us. We decided to pack our outfit over the portage and line our empty boat down to the foot of the rapids. That was quite a job. While we were lining our boat with a long rope, we saw a big scow coming, loaded with a big outfit and three men. We yelled to them "Whitehorse," but they didn't pay any attention to us and went on ahead down the rapids. They bumped into a rock and in five minutes that was the last of them. We never found a trace.

It was early July when they pitched their tent and unloaded their supplies on the Dawson beach. Piska went alone to the creeks to look over the mining claims while Pozza and the others took in the city sights. "We weren't worrying at all. We had lots of grub. All we had to do was cook and eat," Pozza recorded in his unpublished autobiography.

When Piska returned from his scouting trip he said he didn't think the opportunities looked good, and told the others they were on their own to start prospecting. He assured them they could return to camp for provisions when necessary. Pozza paired up with Jack Greer, and George left the party.

The two hopeful young men set out on foot until they reached Discovery on Dominion Creek. There they met a man who showed them how to stake a claim, and advised them to take No. 6 Below on Dominion.

"I blazed a tree, and told Jack to write on the tree that we claimed five hundred feet for placer mining," Pozza recalled. "Jack thought the claim was too wide and was looking for a narrower place, but he did the writing since I could not read or write English.

"We went down the creek, but the prospects were not looking good. I told Jack we better go back to No. 6. When we got there, another fellow had staked our claim because Jack had written: 'I Jack Greer claim twenty acres of this ground for a moose pasture.' A year later the claim sold for thirty-six thousand dollars to the Bank of Commerce in Dawson."

Soon after the incident on Dominion Creek, Greer pulled out of the party and Pozza was left with the old man. "I got some grub and started out once more," Pozza said. He got as far as Monte Cristo Gulch, where a man helped him stake a claim. Eager to begin mining, Pozza returned to the camp only to find an empty tent and a fifty-pound bag of flour — that was all that remained of the four-thousand-dollar outfit they had packed in to Dawson.

Pozza, destitute and homeless, told his story to the Royal Canadian Mounted Police. They offered him money, but Pozza said he would rather have food.

"We are scarce of grub," the captain told him, "but you can join the force."

Pozza, who was short in stature, took a look at those six-foot-tall Mounties and said he was too short. The Mountie measured him at five feet seven inches.

"You're tall enough," he said.

Emil Pozza signed up for a year of special duty. His first job was with a party of surveyors traveling to Fort Yukon. When they reached their destination, the men built a cabin for the crew and got supplies from the nearby Northern Commercial Company store. "We were living like gentlemen in the winter of 1897-98," said Pozza.

After Pozza's year with the Mounties, he got a stake and went prospecting up the McQuestion River to Agart Creek, a three-hundred-mile trek into the wilderness. Along the way his burro fell down a twenty-foot cliff and died, and his two pack horses ran off. Undaunted, Pozza trudged back to Dawson with plans to return to Agart Creek in the fall.

When the creeks and rivers were frozen, Pozza and three other fellows started on the long journey. "We had four dogs and a thousand pounds of provisions," he wrote. "We were so exhausted that we camped on the river ice near Stewart City, but during the night the river overflowed and drove us out on short notice. In those days Stewart City had two saloons, a clothing store, and a Mountie station."

When the group was two days out of Stewart City, they realized they had not obtained a listing of vacant claims on Agart Creek, and there was no commissioner up ahead. Someone had to go back to Stewart City to get the listing.

"I volunteered," Pozza said. He made the trip to Stewart City without difficulty. When he started back, it was thirty-five below. Three miles from camp the river ice broke under Pozza's feet.

I was in water up to my waist and alone. I got out of the water, but my matches were wet. There was no way to start a fire. I took my knife and cut off my socks and moccasins. The sleeves of my mackinaw coat were dry. I cut them off and put them on my feet.

Just before I reached camp, I stepped into an overflow and got my feet wet again. I thought I was apt to succumb right there. I began to shout in hopes that my partners would hear me. Much to my relief they came running to help. They carried me to the tent and did all they could, but I was suffering greatly. By morning I could not move. My partners carried me back to Stewart City, and then they went on to Agart Creek.

In two weeks I got so I could walk with the help of a cane. Wick Nolen, the owner of the roadhouse, said I could stay there as long as I wanted. I told him I was short of cash. "Well," he said, "you can help me by doing some cooking and some of the chores." I stayed there until the spring of 1899. I left for Dawson just before the ice broke up.

By this time Pozza had been in the Klondike nearly two years, and had little to show for his time. "I had an eight-by-ten-foot cabin on the hillside, but I was suffering all the time from the effects of my accident on the river. That went on for three years," he wrote. He was forced to take menial jobs, working as a porter at the Fairview and the Monte Cristo Hotel.

One day a fellow came to me and told me he had a candy store and would like me to go into business with him. I told him I could buy nothing, and furthermore, I was sick. He told me that was the reason he wanted to help me. I went to see his place of business. He had a small cigar stand and some fresh fruit, and he was making candy which he sold wholesale to other retailers. "You won't have to have cash to get interested with me," this fellow said. "You can pay as you go along."

I took him up on his proposition. We did a nice business for the size of the investment. One day he said to me, "If we had a few thousand dollars, we could double our money in no time." His idea was to get more stock so we could increase our volume. It sounded like a good idea to me. I went to my friend, Joseph, and told him we needed money to expand our candy business. "How much do you want?" he asked. About seventy-five hundred dollars, I told him.

Joseph got a big gold poke and let me have the amount in gold dust. My partner took the next boat to San Francisco, where he purchased butter, cream, eggs and other perishables for candy making, and had them shipped to Dawson. When our goods got to Seattle the longshoremen were on strike, and our perishables sat spoiling on the dock while the strike was being settled. By the time it finally reached Dawson, the food was nearly ruined. My partner had enough money to pay his half of the loan, but I did not. I got disgusted and quit the business, and went to work for Joseph until he was paid in full.

By the time Emil Pozza worked off his debt, it was the fall of 1905. Dawson had peaked and it was time to move on. News of the Fairbanks strike prompted him to go to Alaska. Pozza was older and wiser, and took care in selecting his partners for a mining venture in the Fairbanks district. With good equipment, including a boiler, they had five successful seasons. Due to Emil's physical ailments, he was unable to work any longer with a pick and shovel. Never too proud to take on any chore, he hired out as a swamper in the Mine Home Saloon in Garden Island.

Although Emil did not give details, his Fairbanks mining venture must have given him a good nest egg because in 1917 he purchased half interest in a brick restaurant in Garden Island. (He also married, but his wife was never mentioned in his manuscript.) "We were doing a land office business at the restaurant for more than a year, when we lost everything in a fire with only one thousand dollars in insurance."

Two years later Emil built the International Hotel, a twenty-room structure which was operating successfully until it was displaced by the railroad.

By the mid 1920s Pozza purchased a piece of property and a building at the corner of First and Lacey for thirty-five hundred dollars. There he operated a second-hand store. Business was good, but five years later he sold out to Austin "Cap" Lathrop for six thousand dollars. Pozza reinvested the money by buying three acres from Mrs. Louis Janson on the outskirts of town. He paid her three hundred dollars. "I put nearly all of it under cultivation. I was doing fine, raising some of the best vegetables in the country."

Two years later a military officer knocked at Pozza's door. The government wanted his land for the location of Ladd Air Force Base (now Fort Wainwright). By then Pozza had built a twenty-five-by-fifty-foot warehouse, four rental cabins, and a cabin for himself.

"I thought I was well off and wouldn't have to worry any more," Pozza said. It seemed he had no choice; he had to sell. He told the military that he would not sell unless he got ten thousand dollars for his property, buildings, and loss of income. Instead, they paid him thirty-nine hundred dollars.

"After they chased me out of Ladd Field," Pozza wrote, "I bought another piece of property for four hundred and fifty dollars. I was sick most of the time, and in and out of St. Joseph's Hospital until my finances were exhausted."

He entered Sitka Pioneer Home in 1945. During the first ten years he worked in the cemetery. In 1967 he transferred to the Fairbanks Pioneer Home, where he died a year later at ninety-seven.

So ends the story of Hard-Luck Pozza.

ROBERT AND JESSIE BLOOM

When Jessie Bloom was twenty-four she came to Fairbanks as the bride of Robert Bloom — Chilkoot climber, Klondike man, and owner of a Fairbanks hardware store which he had established soon after his arrival in 1904. His roots were in Lithuania, hers in Ireland, and somehow they met and married in London in 1912.

The house they called home, where their four daughters were reared, was a long, boxcar-shaped frame building originally located on Third Avenue between Cushman and Lacey. It now stands empty and uprooted in the 1200 block on Second Avenue. Aluminum siding disguises the age of the house, which was built more than sixty-seven years ago. The windows are still intact and inside one can see the old-fashioned wallpaper that brightened the living room in days gone by. Within its walls, beneath the creaky, leaky roof are secrets we will never know. It sets one to wondering.

The heart of that house was a wood-burning Mallable kitchen stove, purchased secondhand at Aroin's furniture store in Seattle in 1912. Every family meal from that time until 1945 was cooked on that stove. It was then replaced by an electric range and the old stove was sold to a miner for its original price.

It is safe to say that in all those years the kitchen stove never went out. Even in the summer there was the need for hot water, so the big teakettle was kept steaming and humming. The sound of the kettle, the delightful aroma of bread baking and a roast in the oven, are the memories of which the Bloom house is made.

We feel fortunate to have come across — thanks to our friends at the University of Alaska Archives — a story on housekeeping

Robert Bloom, from Lithuania, and Jessie, from Ireland, were married in London and reared four daughters in pioneer Fairbanks.

written by Mrs. Bloom. For a young woman from Dublin, there were many adjustments to be made. She set about adapting herself to being a pioneer wife.

For example, water was purchased from the water wagon, which made its round each day — on wheels in the summer, runners in the winter — for ten cents for two five-gallon cans. There was a wood-burning stove on the water wagon to keep the water from freezing, and on the stove was a coffee pot. It was not unusual to see the water man sipping hot coffee between deliveries.

"We could get extra water in the winter by going to the river and cutting chunks of ice and melting that," wrote Mrs. Bloom. "The river water was much softer than the well water. We sometimes melted snow, but it took so much to get even a pint of water that we did not do it often. Almost everyone had a rain barrel and we saved rain water for special purposes, like shampooing hair and washing baby diapers."

In those days flour and sugar came in one-hundred-pound cotton sacks, and the sacks were used for dish towels, pillow cases or aprons. One of Mrs. Bloom's neighbors decorated sugar sacks with hemstitching and hung them as curtains.

Food was kept cool in the cellar. Access was through a trap door in the kitchen floor. If a homemaker was not efficient, she would be opening and closing that trap door many times a day, wearing herself out and letting cold air into the house.

"We learned to freeze things we had not thought of freezing before," she recalled. "We baked bread in batches to last a week, froze it and thawed it as we needed it."

Before the railroad was built, supplies were shipped in during the summer when the rivers were navigable. Canned vegetables and fruits were a mainstay, and rare was the household without a sack of dried apples. "We always had applesauce made from the dried apples. We had it frozen on the back porch, in chunks, and when we needed a dessert we brought in a chunk."

Wood fueled all the stoves in the Bloom house. "During the winter one side of the living room was stacked with logs. During the sub-zero days Bob kept the logs piled almost to the ceiling. The fires were going continuously from the first cold snap in November until the end of April. The wood deposited creosote in the tin smokestacks, which was a fire hazard. Every Sunday morning we cleaned the chimneys. I don't think there was any time of the day that we were not conscious of fire prevention."

Housekeeping without any modern conveniences took longer and "there was never a free moment until the children were in bed," Jessie said. "At night the children loved to listen to phonograph records. I would play them until the children were settled down. There were no shortcuts. Even playing records required concentration. You had to place each record on the machine and take it off when it was finished. Mere living took so much from one, yet when there was a free moment, one just gloried in it."

EVA McGOWN, Irish Legend

Eva McGown left an indelible mark on the town. I see her now, leaving the Nordale Hotel on her way to the post office, decked out in a smart, dark suit with a corsage of silk flowers on her shoulder, a hat upon her head, and high heels in the snow. There is a dignified sashay to her walk, and in her wake the fragrance of violets. She never ventured from her room without Yardley's violet perfume generously applied to wrist and throat.

On this day of remembering the color is high in her cheeks, her blue eyes sparkle, and wisps of silver hair poke out from beneath her hat. She stops to greet people and it takes half an hour to walk the short block to the post office. Her voice is lilting; the words spill and trill, thick with an Irish brogue. Her laughter carries like the ringing of little silver bells.

For a good many of Eva's fifty-eight years in Fairbanks she was the city hostess, paid a very small salary. To her it was more than a job, it was a way of life to do for others — to help newcomers find lodgings, visit the sick, cheer the lonely, comfort the sorrowful.

During World War II Eva took it upon herself to persuade residents who had extra rooms to take in people with no place to live. She had a knack for bringing the right people together, and enough charm to coax the birds out of the trees. The city put her on the payroll — at a mere one hundred fifty dollars annually — as housing and employment agent.

Her office, a small desk in a corner of the Nordale Hotel lobby, was a gathering place for homesick servicemen, transient workers, and old-timers who needed someone to talk to. Eva also greeted dignitaries at the airport and was a vivacious and unforgettable ambassador. She put Fairbanks on the map as the Golden Heart City of Alaska, and in recognition of her work the governor named

Eva McGown, honorary hostess of Alaska — through fifty-eight years of pioneering, she never ceased to be a gentlewoman.

her honorary hostess of the Territory.

When the City of Fairbanks gave Eva a gold watch for her many years of service, she said that the bread she cast on the water "came back with butter and jam on it."

Born in Belfast, County Antrim, North Ireland, in 1883, Eva Montgomery was reared to enjoy the finer things of life. In her father's house she presided at formal teas with sterling silver service and the most delicate of china cups. She wore seven petticoats beneath her muslin frock, and carried a silk parasol to shade her from the sun.

In 1914 she left Ireland for love of Arthur Louis McGown, and came to Fairbanks to be married. She was thirty-one. Eva tells about the trip in a *Reader's Digest* story published in 1951. "It took me more than a month overland [from Valdez] to Fairbanks by horse and dogsled in bitter cold, staying by night in roadhouses that were only shacks, and never warm. There were blizzards, too, that held us in a roadhouse for days, me alone with those men, lucky to have a room of my own, with a tin bowl to bathe from.

"All those rough men were kind. Never a cursing word did they say in my hearing. They gave me hot bricks for my feet, and wrapped fur around me."

Eva and Arthur were married in February, 1914. They lived in a three-room frame cottage, which is still standing at the corner of Sixth and Ferry. While Arthur managed his business — he owned the Model Cafe — Eva taught school.

They had five good years before Arthur became ill. The time came when he could no longer work and was in constant pain. Eva nursed him full-time. To her fell the jobs of chopping wood, hauling water and shoveling snow. Eva was widowed in 1930 and never remarried.

When she could no longer afford to live in the house she moved into a room at the Nordale, where she stayed for twenty-seven years. The room was small, too small to accommodate Eva's style of living, but she never gave up trying. She delighted in serving her friends sherry in eggshell-thin stemware imported from Italy, and tea in hand-painted china cups, which she washed in a small wall-hung sink.

She took most of her meals in restaurants and cafes near the hotel, but in the morning she had her tea and porridge, cooked in her room on a two-burner hot plate on the windowsill. Never did she succumb to instant oatmeal or instant tea.

And speaking of tea, Eva was not one bit bashful about instructing the waitresses on the proper method of making it.

"You must heat the teapot first," she insisted. "Then pour the boiling water — I said boiling, mind you — over the tea."

Pleasing Eva was one of the nicest things that could happen to anyone's day. Her happiness was contagious.

Visitors to Eva's room were treated like royalty and were so caught up in her artful patter that it did not matter that there was no place to sit. The bed was stacked with clothes and boxes and newspapers and books. So was the chair, the table, the floor. There was a narrow trail — not without obstructions — around the bed and to the sink, which she navigated with some difficulty as the years slipped by.

She had long outgrown the tiny room, but that did not faze Eva. She continued to add to the contents. Her friends did not help matters; they gave her gifts — jewelry, scarves, gloves. There was no place to put them except on top of things, or under the bed, and so the piles grew, here, there and everywhere.

Eva's guests left her room with hearts uplifted, and gifts pressed into their hands — a jar of orange marmalade from Scotland, a box of lemon drops, a book of verse, a lace handkerchief, and words of wisdom. Her generosity overflowed, the generosity of a loving heart that puts another's pleasure before one's own.

Eva had a faith that was as natural as breathing. She talked to God — and about Him — as her dearest friend. There was no fear in Eva; she was indomitable. She was ageless. She had the vivacity and sweetness of a young girl. When she was eighty-eight, the last year of her life, she fussed about her hair, her face powder, her lipstick and the color of her gloves. And she never gave up wearing perfume. The sweet fragrance of violets hovered around her like a band of angels.

In 1967, when the waters of the Chena River came rolling over the banks and spilling three feet of water into the lobby of the Nordale, Eva was carried to safety in the arms of a young man. For several weeks she lived in the University of Alaska dormitory, eating French pastries sent to her by friends in Seattle. After the flood had subsided, she returned to her room at the hotel, and to her good works.

There was a sign above Eva's desk which said: "Do it now." That was the motto by which she lived, and by the instructions in the Good Book and by her own wit and wisdom.

On February 22, 1972, Eva had dinner downtown with a friend and returned to her room about nine o'clock. Very shortly thereafter the fire alarm sounded in the hotel. Smoke and flames erupted from a ground-floor room and soon filled the upper stories. Eva attempted to leave her room, but was forced back by the smoke and fire. The old building — of dry timbers with sawdust insulation — went up like a torch.

Her call for help was enough to wake a man in a nearby room. He tried to save her, but the smoke and flames were too thick.

Amid the ashes of the Nordale was the hotel safe, which contained a small box belonging to Eva McGown. Inside were a wee bit of soil and a few pieces of dried moss — a little bit of Ireland that Eva had kept with her all those years.

C.W. ADAMS, Steamboat Man

This story about C.W. Adams is based on his autobiography,
A Cheekchako Goes to the Klondike.

Charles Adams was a country boy from North Dakota. At twenty-four he set out for the Klondike. He was one of the 98ers who hefted pack on back and conquered Chilkoot. It took seven trips to get his eight hundred pounds of supplies over the pass.

His first experience with boats was building an eighteen-foot vessel of spruce on the shores of Lake Lindemann. Adams and his crew caulked the seams with torn flour sacks and melted spruce pitch. Wonder of wonders, the scow floated — all the way down the Yukon River to Dawson's front door.

"Sometimes we would walk around Dawson," Adams wrote, "and go into the saloons and dance halls and gambling places. I did not dance, and had never tasted any kind of liquor nor gambled. I was very bashful — if one of the dance-hall girls had spoken to me, I would have fainted."

Adams wanted to find gold, but he was cheated out of one piece of property by a clerk in the recording office, and thwarted by a payless hold on another claim. He never turned down an opportunity to work. A dollar-an-hour job at a sawmill was better than nothing. In the fall Adams and a friend went moose hunting and took their kill to meat-starved Dawson, where a restaurant man paid five hundred dollars for it — hide, antlers and all.

The LaVelle Young, *Capt. C.W. Adams, carried the first cargo up the Chena in 1901, and determined the location of Fairbanks.*

By November Charles was discouraged and restless. He yearned for home. He joined a party of travelers going over White Pass to Skagway. "I think the distance from Dawson to Skagway is four hundred miles," Adams wrote, "and in all that trip none of us ever had a cold or became ill in any way. But the next day after reaching Skagway, we all caught colds." The trip took twenty days.

In the spring of 1899 Charles longed to go north again. His brother staked him to a second Klondike venture, and this time Adams, with a partner, bought one hundred fifty tons of fresh vegetables and fruit — oranges, apples, lemons — and eggs, plus enough lumber to build a scow, and set sail for Dawson.

The fresh produce sold faster than sourdough hotcakes in scurvy-ridden Dawson. With their earnings Adams and his partner bought a mine sixteen miles up Bonanza Creek on Gold Hill. But there was one problem. It was a hillside claim which had caved in and could not be worked until winter, when the tunnel was frozen. In the meantime, one hundred cords of wood were needed to fuel the thawing in the mine. The partner, not liking the idea of all that work, sold out to Adams.

"There I was with seven dollars and fifty cents, a little grub, and all that wood to cut," Charles wrote. "I knew I would need to hire horses to haul the wood to the claim, and I would need hay for the horses." Fortunately, there was a lot of wild grass on the hillside. Adams hired a helper, and "we set to work with a butcher knife. We would take large handfuls of grass, cut it off, and spread it out to dry. After drying, we tied the hay up in bundles . . . and then made stacks until we figured we had three tons."

When Adams finally began tunneling, there was so much gas in the tunnel that he had to buy a steam boiler to do the thawing instead of open burning. To pay for the equipment, Adams took a partner. Then they hit it big. "The pay dirt kept getting richer and richer. One day we took out a good-sized quartz rock worth four hundred and twenty-two dollars," Adams wrote.

At that time the going rate in Dawson for mine workers was a dollar an hour, and the men had to furnish their own food.

"They stayed in my cabin," Charles said. "We all took turns cooking. The main thing was, of course, bacon and beans. We worked ten hours a day."

By the following summer, after sluicing their dump, Adams and his partner cleaned up $127,000. Since the mine was worked out, Adams decided to go on the Nome stampede, but before leaving

Dawson he bought a claim on Trail Creek for four thousand dollars.

Adams — with a pocketful of money — landed on the black sands of Nome in June, 1900. There were no hotel accommodations available, so he bought a tent and camped on the beach with the horde of stampeders, many of them from the Dawson diggings.

Charles had no luck in staking a claim in that rush, but he met two friends, Tom Bruce and George Crummy, who proposed they become partners and buy a riverboat to make the run between Nome and Dawson.

The boat could more than pay for itself on one trip with a load of passengers and freight, Bruce reasoned. He knew of a boat which could be purchased for twenty thousand dollars. She was the steamer *LaVelle Young,* anchored at St. Michael. Tom had fifteen hundred dollars and George had eight hundred, which meant Adams would have to put up the rest.

"Anyone with the least bit of common sense would have had nothing to do with that kind of deal," Adams wrote, "especially when we knew absolutely nothing about steamboating. But I agreed. We bought the boat from an agent in Nome, paying half down. It was the middle of August, and we figured we should leave for Dawson on September 1."

Adams put an advertisement in the Nome newspaper.

While they waited for the customers to come, they lined up a crew and hired a captain, a pilot, and first and second engineers. Adams was the purser; George, the second mate, and Tom the steward.

"We didn't know anything about the men we hired, especially the officers," Adams wrote. "The captain brought aboard a five-gallon jug of whiskey and got drunk — so we let him go, and looked for another one."

By the time the *LaVelle Young* was ready, there were one hundred passengers at one hundred twenty-five dollars each, and one hundred tons of freight at one hundred dollars a ton. They traveled successfully through the salty Bering Sea and into the Yukon River. At that point they had to anchor to cool down the boiler and wash the salt out of it. After the washing, the boiler had to be heated slowly to get the steam up — a process that took about twenty hours.

"The crew cut quite a lot of wood for our boiler," Adams said. "I helped, and so did the passengers — those who could tear themselves away from gambling, which went on all the time."

Once the *LaVelle Young* was under way, they traveled one hundred thirty miles until a leak was discovered in the boiler, caused by getting the steam up too fast after washing it.

"The engineer said the boiler was useless," Adams wrote, "and we could go no farther."

The next day the steamer *Sarah* came along and took the *LaVelle Young* passengers and freight to Dawson. It had been a costly trip for Adams and his partners. While Bruce and Crummy took the damaged vessel back to St. Michael to put her in winter quarters, Adams went on to Dawson and Seattle, where he met Captain Betts to pay the ten-thousand-dollar balance owing on the *LaVelle Young*.

"Captain Betts was very fair," Adams said. "He said he knew we had had very bad luck with the steamer and would accept five thousand dollars as full payment."

To recoup their losses, Adams had to buy a new boiler, get it to St. Michael, and install it. Adams' brother, Howard, decided to accompany him back to Dawson. They hauled in twenty tons of goods. "We got a good price for everything." In the meantime, Adams' other brother, George, chartered a sailing vessel, loaded her with coal and the new boiler, and set out for St. Michael. After installing the boiler, they went to Nome and sold the coal — thereby paying for the boiler.

"We soon had the *LaVelle Young* ready and got a load of three hundred tons of general merchandise to take back to Dawson," Adams said.

He wintered the steamer in a slough above Dawson while he and his brother Howard worked the mine on Trail Creek. When spring came, Adams took the *LaVelle* to St. Michael where he met Capt. E.T. Barnette, waiting for a shipment of goods from Seattle. Barnette intended to transport his stock up the Tanana aboard his steamer *Arctic Boy*. In July Barnette struck a rock and his steamer sank. He then asked Adams to take him up the Tanana River to Tanana Crossing.

"None of us had ever been up the Tanana," Adams said.

He had been told by other steamer captains that it was doubtful the *LaVelle* could get beyond the mouth of Chena Slough. Adams made a contract with Barnette to take him and one hundred thirty tons of goods to the mouth of the slough for a certain price per ton, and for an additional sum, to Tanana Crossing. On board were Mrs. Barnette, four men, a dog team and a horse. They departed St. Michael on August 8.

"It was also agreed that if we got beyond the Chena Slough and could go no farther, Barnette would get off with his goods wherever that happened to be," Adams wrote.

For eighteen days they steamed on the Yukon, the Tanana and the Chena, cutting dry wood for the boiler as needed, until they reached a point above where Fairbanks is now located.

"I then told Captain Barnette that according to the contract he should get off here, but he wanted me to take him to the mouth of the slough," Adams wrote. "He said he had noticed a high, heavily wooded bank about six miles below, and asked me to take him there. I agreed to do so."

They tied up at four o'clock on August 26, 1901, on the Chena where the Nordstrom building stands today.

An hour later Angus McDougall, a deckhand, cut the first tree to make a clearing to pile Barnette's goods on shore. The second day, while they were unloading, two prospectors came along and became the first customers at Barnette's trading post. One of the prospectors was Felix Pedro.

"It looked very bad for Captain Barnette to be put off there with no Indians or anyone to trade with," Adams wrote. "Mrs. Barnette was crying when we left the next day, as it did not look good to her either.

"Captain Barnette was angry with me because I would not take him to the south of the slough, but late that winter I saw him in Dawson on his way outside and he was all smiles. He said I could not have put him off in a better place!"

It didn't take Adams long to realize that steamboating at its best "is nothing but trouble," and he had his share of it with the *LaVelle Young.* He sold her to the Alaska Commerical Company for fifteen thousand dollars, intending to stay out of that business, but his good intentions did not last long. In the spring of 1904 he bought the one-hundred-seventy-five-foot vessel *Oil City* for seventy-five hundred dollars, and ordered a barge from Seattle to increase the freight capacity.

"Why should I have been so foolish as to buy another boat?" Adams lamented.

Oil City was no bed of roses. The first season, with a load of passengers sixty miles up the Tanana River, the wheel shaft broke. "This was a terrible accident," Charles wrote. "The steamer *Cudahy* came along on the way to Fairbanks and took all our passengers, which cost me quite a lot." The barge he had ordered from Seattle was lost in a storm crossing the Gulf of Alaska, another devastating blow.

"Seemed I was having nothing but trouble," Charles said.

Since some big expenditures were needed to repair the *Oil City*, Adams had to take a partner who invested six thousand dollars. They ordered a six-ton hollow steel shaft from the East Coast. When the shaft arrived in Whitehorse, Adams' partner had to freight the equipment to Lake Lebarge. There he built a scow, got the six tons on board, and when the ice left the lakes and rivers, he made his way to Dawson.

Meanwhile, a new barge was being built at St. Michael. The carpenter followed the blueprints drawn up by the captain, but was leery of the plans because there was no allowance for keelsons (a set of timbers fastened inside the hull of the ship along the keel for structural strength); instead, there were only props to hold up the deck.

"The ship with our freight came into the harbor," Adams wrote, "and we went alongside with the *Oil City* and began loading the barge. Nothing is put in the holds of these river barges — everything is stowed on the deck. The barge was two-thirds loaded when there was a great crash. The whole bridge shook. The deckhands came running as the barge slowly sank. Without any solid keelson to hold the deck up, it caved in."

The barge was towed to a sloping beach. As each tide came in, Adams managed to move the barge to higher ground and unload the freight.

That fall Adams took the *Oil City* to Dawson for winter storage.

The following year, when the freighting season was over and the *Oil City* safely wintered at Chena, Adams was anxious to get to Dawson. It was early November, 1906, and the trail was four hundred miles long by way of the overland route to Circle and up the frozen Yukon. Charles teamed up with Henry Isaaks, a Fairbanks clothing merchant. They bought a horse and sleigh to make traveling easier.

"We got oats and hay for the horse and very little in the line of grub for ourselves, as we could find roadhouses along the trail," Adams said. "We did take a couple of blankets, and Henry had a gallon of whiskey."

They made Chatanika the first evening. By the next day a wet, heavy snow was falling, making travel difficult. They were forced to stop early and make camp at a deserted miner's cabin. "Henry was not used to walking. He sat in the sled while I walked ahead with the horses," Adams said. "I was wearing moccasins and could feel where the trail was under the snow. Henry drank whiskey when we stopped at night. He could never understand why I would not have any. Water or tea was all I wanted. I had never tasted liquor."

The weather was very cold the next day when they left Cold Creek. "We were going along minding our business, when all at once the horse broke through the ice and went into the river with just his head above water. Fortunately the sleigh did not break through. I grabbed the horse's bridle and held on while Henry unhitched him.

"By that time the poor little horse was very cold and did not want to move. We had to switch him with a stout willow to get him going. It was lucky that the sleigh stayed up — it had six thousand dollars in gold dust on it, and gold dust is very heavy."

That night in a deserted cabin, there was food for the horse, whiskey for Isaaks, but nothing for Adams to eat. He had all that gold, but not even a bite of bacon, beans or bread.

The year 1907 was a good year. Adams and his *Oil City* partners freighted with two one-hundred-fifty-foot barges on the St. Michael-Dawson-Fairbanks run. At season's end he said, "The freight money more than paid for all the disasters we had." Not wanting to tempt fate, Charles got out of the steamboat business and bought a mining claim on Vault Creek, twenty miles from Fairbanks. He and his partner, Bert Walker, built a cookhouse, bunkhouse and boiler-house. They hired two men and sank a shaft one hundred eighty feet — all hand-digging.

By February, 1908, they finally reached bedrock but found no pay. Adams and his partner got discouraged and sold out. The new owner hit pay and quickly took out fifteen thousand dollars. "I guess that's the way things happen in gold mining," Adams said. "Now I didn't have a mine or a steamboat."

In the spring of 1909 he hired out as purser on the *Julia B,* traveling from Chena to St. Michael. That fall, at thirty-four, he married Elizabeth McComb in Fairbanks. Charles wrote very little about his wife and married life.

"I never could stay idle very long," Charles wrote, "and in early November I got the silly notion of going to Twelve Mile to cut cord-wood for the river steamers. When I spoke to Elizabeth about it, she said it was all right with her — so down I went."

He cut a fine stand of spruce and built a one-room cabin caulked with moss. Elizabeth came to live with him in the forest, where he cut fifty cords of wood. "Since it was too early to go back to Fairbanks," he said, "I cut another sixteen cords. One morning it was sixty-five below, and the air was very still. Wood splits so easily at that temperature that I could not stop chopping. The trees were frozen solid, and just one blow from the ax would split a four-foot length as easy as butter."

That spring Adams went to Fairbanks to get his master's license so he could be hired as a captain. He had been a steamboat man for ten years, and knew the rivers better than most captains. The Natives called Adams "Owl Eyes — the man who can see in the dark."

In 1911 Charles got the challenging job of piloting the steamer *Minneapolis* and her barge. It was a challenge because the boat and barge were frozen in the Yukon thirty miles above Ruby. "There was about as much chance of saving the vessel during breakup as jumping over the moon," Adams said. "I could see no way of saving the boat and barge from the onslaught of the tons of moving ice, other than to haul them out. For that I needed at least three heavy blocks and tackles, and would have to sink a deadman [log]. It would be a very big job, and of course we had no tackle."

Adams located tackle at an old Army post up the Tanana. On his return trip he happened to talk to a mail carrier who had seen many spring breakups on the Yukon. He told Adams that when the weather got warm enough to start melting the ice, the river would start to rise an inch an hour. The ice in the deep water would rise with the water, but the ice next to the shore was frozen to the ground and would not come up until much later. Until then there would be a narrow channel of water three and a half feet deep next to the shore. If Adams could move upstream in that channel and get behind a certain island, the steamer would be protected from the tons of ice — some pieces as big as two-story buildings — that came thundering downstream propelled by the mighty Yukon current.

Adams prepared for his flight to safe harbor by making the *Minneapolis* as light as possible. "We got our steam up," he said. "Old Man River began coming up an inch an hour. We were all watching it. The next day we pulled the boat and barge — by means of block and tackle — to shore and into the narrow channel. The following day we backed our way very slowly upstream. We had to be very careful not to start the shore ice from coming up. We made it around the first bluff, when a big piece of ice came up between the boat and barge. There was nothing to do but tie the barge securely ashore, and continue backing down with the boat. Unfortunately, the wind had blown a lot of heavy snow into the river. I thought we could back through it, but we got stuck, and stuck hard. What to do? Well, there was nothing we could do but wait for the rise of the water to set us free.

"That night I did not sleep — just paced the deck, watching the river. Eventually it lifted us up and out, so the next afternoon we backed down almost to the bluff. We reached the eddy just in time! All of a sudden the shore ice came up. We were as safe as if in dry dock. In several hours all the ice began to move, and it never stopped. It was a wonderful sight to see — all that ice moving and breaking up."

The people up and down the river who said that nothing could save the *Minneapolis* had changed their tune. In a few days, when the river was free of ice, Adams took the steamer to Tanana where he picked up thirty tons of freight for the Iditarod miners.

In the spring of 1912 Captain Adams' first run was with the steamer *Julia B* on a twelve-hundred-mile run from St. Michael to Fairbanks with a load of fresh fruits and vegetables — a most welcome cargo to townspeople who had survived the winter on dried prunes and canned beets. It was a holiday crowd that thronged the waterfront to welcome the first steamboat of the season. Adams looked down on a scene he had witnessed many times before — the upturned faces of men and women anxious to spot a loved one among the passengers, of tradesmen eager for supplies, of children delighted at the novelty of the ship's arrival. It was like a hero's homecoming — a brief moment of glory in a less than glamorous occupation.

In 1917 Captain Adams noted that times were changing on the river, with the big companies such as the White Pass buying out the independent steamboat owners. The White Pass hired Adams to operate their passenger boat *Alaska* between Whitehorse and Dawson.

Several years later, the steamboat era was drawing to a close. With the completion of the Alaska Railroad in 1923, freight was shipped by boat to Seward and by rail to the Interior. A few steamboats remained in Nenana to supply Yukon River villages. Adams was hired as master of the ARR's newly constructed steamer *Nenana*, a two-hundred-ten-foot wood-burning sternwheeler which consumed a cord of wood an hour and required a crew of thirty-two. The *Nenana* is included in the National Register of Historic Places and can be seen at Alaskaland in Fairbanks.

Elizabeth had died. In 1933 Charles married Helen St. George. During the next ten years they lived in Alaska during the summer while Charles piloted boats on the Interior rivers. In the winter they lived in California. The 1946 season was Adams' last one on the river. His career as a steamboat man spanned forty-five years. He retired at age seventy.

FANNIE THE HIKE

She was quick on the trigger, she could wrestle a bear, she could outsmart a wolf, and she could out-drink and out-cuss just about any man in the North.

She was Alaska's answer to Annie Oakley, the hundred-pound female counterpart of Dan'l Boone, Davie Crockett and assorted other folk heroes of frontier years in the Lower 48.

Her roots were in a Bohemian settlement in Nebraska, where she was born in 1871. She never had formal schooling, she didn't learn to speak English until she was grown up, yet she was widely read and could hold her own in any conversation.

She was twenty-seven when she joined the stampede of '98, a bundle of energy with a pack on her back. A Yukon stove, some bacon, beans and flour were her stock in trade. "I reckon I've set up my tent and hung my Meals-for-Sale sign at most every strike in the North," she said. She reached most of those strikes on foot and thus earned her handle, "Fannie the Hike."

She settled finally, in the Kantishna, as the wife but definitely not the dependent of Joe Quigley. She mined, hunted, mushed dogs, trapped, and welcomed any traveler who came into the rugged country there in the shadow of Mount McKinley. A surprising number did come — park rangers, Geological Survey crews, big-game hunters, climbers. The unique Sourdough Expedition of 1910, the Belmore Browne party, defeated by a blizzard in 1912, the Stuck-Karsten group who made the first climb on both peaks in 1913, were the first but not the last climbers to experience Fannie's hospitality.

Joe Quigley crossed Chilkoot as early as 1893, and prospected the Fortymile and Circle before the Klondike strike. He was on the scene for the Fairbanks gold rush in 1903, and it was there his path merged with Fannie's. He was sick with typhoid fever when they met, and she nursed him back to health. Joe married her in 1906, knowing she was an independent woman.

Joe made his strike in the Kantishna. Ore from his Red Top Mine contained gold and silver. It was taken by dog team to the Kantishna River, floated to Nenana, then transported by rail to Seward and by barge to Tacoma, Washington — a two-thousand-mile trip from mine to smelter. Not a get-rich-quick venture, nor an easy way to make a living.

Fannie, dressed in men's trousers, a heavy shirt, a black slicker and an old sou'wester, tackled the challenge of making a living in the wilderness with zest. She raised a garden, in a region that has only ten frost-free weeks a year. She bagged all the meat she and Joe ate or served their drop-in guests. She rendered bear fat into lard for a crust worthy of her famous blueberry pie. She ran a trapline, and mushed her dogs twenty miles for firewood. Mail call, in those early days, was once a year.

The Quigleys had one neighbor, "Little Johnnie" Busia, a miner from Croatia who lived a mile away on Moose Creek. One of Little Johnnie's several claims to fame was his home brew, called Kantishna champagne. Fannie like it so well she kept a bottle of it tucked inside her boot.

One fall when Fannie was out hunting, she spotted a caribou bull that suited her needs. Just as she took aim and fired, the bull moved behind a clump of trees. It wasn't often that Fannie missed. The bull reappeared, or so she thought. She shot again. Two bulls, both wounded, leaped out of the brush and charged into Moose Creek. The water was about four feet deep, and running with slush ice. When the caribou were halfway across, both dropped dead.

Many hunters would have left the meat in the creek and gone looking for another caribou. Not Fannie. She tied a rope to both carcasses and secured it to a tree to keep them from floating downstream. Then, working in the ice-laden water, she pushed and pulled, cursed and shoved, until she got both carcasses ashore. It never occurred to her to go for help. She skinned and butchered the meat and took it home. A very independent woman.

Another year Fannie was moose-hunting, alone, as usual. It was late in the season, and cold, and almost dark by the time she spotted a moose. It was in high country, with few trees and no place to take shelter. If she shot the moose and left it unattended overnight, the bears and wolves would have a fine feast on her meat. If she let the moose go she might not get a second chance, and she needed the meat to get through the winter.

Fannie killed the moose with a single shot, gutted it in the fading light, and solved the problem of where to spend the night by crawling inside the warm carcass. The carcass froze while Fannie slept, and she "had a heckova time" cutting her way out. At least that's the way she liked to tell it, embellished with a few choice cusswords. Edna Ferber heard the story when she visited Fairbanks, and liked it so well she included it in her book, *Ice Palace.*

By 1926 Alaskans were taking to the air in small planes, which saved many a weary mile of walking or mushing dogs. One day when Joe was in Fairbanks, he decided to fly home and save himself the long, arduous overland trip. Fannie, waiting alone at the cabin, heard the roar of the plane overhead. It ended in a loud crash. She rushed out and reached the wreckage in time to see her husband crawling out, blood running down his front from a gash in his nose.

"It was split clean through lengthwise," Fannie said. "I got out my needle and catgut, washed 'em, and sewed up his nose. That was the first time I ever sewed up a person, and I sewed him the way I do my moccasins, with a baseball stitch." The nose healed.

Grant Pearson, a park ranger and then superintendent of Mount McKinley National Park, knew Fannie well and had some good stories about her. One he told in his book, *My Life of High Adventure,* was about the time Father Fitzgerald and his pilot made a forced landing on the gravel bar near the Quigley cabin. Fannie, always hospitable, invited the men to the cabin, served them her famous caribou stew and blueberry pie, and gave them a place to sleep.

Two days later, when weather permitted and the men were ready to leave, Father Fitzgerald asked Fannie, "How much do I owe you?"

"You don't owe me anything," she said. "We're glad to have you, any time."

"Well, then, after we get to Fairbanks, my pilot will be flying back here. What kind of chocolates do you like?"

"Schlitz," Fannie answered without batting an eye.

Next day the pilot returned with two cases of Schlitz beer and a quart of whiskey.

There was another side to Fannie, unexpected to those who knew her for her outdoor skills, her total frankness and her appetite for Kantishna champagne. Besides the lettuce and radishes, turnips, cabbages and such needed for their table, Fannie grew flowers. Wrote Grant Pearson ["Fannie the Hike," *The Alaska Sportsman®*, August 1947] ". . . pansies were her favorites, and for her they grew to unbelievable size. She took notes on their colors, dried them, and reproduced them in needlework in the exact colors Nature had chosen. You felt like touching the embroidered one to make sure it wasn't the original pansy." So the "baseball stitch" she used on Joe's split nose wasn't the only stitch she knew.

"To some of those who visited her, Fannie was a sort of curiosity," Pearson wrote, "which according to ordinary standards she was, indeed. But she was more . . . genuine, sincere, a truly great personality."

Money, the motive that had propelled both Fannie and Joe to the North, had long since lost its importance in their lives, replaced by a desire to live in harmony with the land which gave them wealth of an intangible kind — wilderness and freedom to roam in it.

Eventually Joe wanted to retire to the softer life of the Lower 48, and eventually he did, but Fannie, her face leathery from exposure, her small body shrunk even smaller with the years, refused to leave her log cabin in the wilderness. Once she fell and broke her hip, and had no choice but to stay in the Fairbanks hospital for several weeks. But as soon as she could walk again she went home, a walking stick in one hand, her rifle in the other, and some Kantishna champagne in her boot top.

Little Johnnie, concerned about Fannie but respectful of her independence, kept a surreptitious watch. "I worry about her," he told Grant Pearson. "She could fall and get hurt, and lie there and freeze to death."

That didn't happen. In August of 1944, at age seventy-three, Fannie the Hike died in her sleep.

Landmarks

Charlie Main's store was a shopper's ark — two of everything, and even Charlie Main didn't always know where to find them.

Landmarks

CHARLIE MAIN'S STORE

In Charlie Main's store, long gone, that stood on the corner of First and Noble Street, a parking lot now, you could buy kerosene lamps with glass chimneys, red-fox skins, safety pins, cooking pots, moose hides, ivory carvings, bullets, baleen baskets, wool socks, silk pajamas, leather mitts, gold nugget bracelets, overcoats, guns, nylon stockings, bear traps, beaded slippers, axes, knives, alarm clocks, long underwear and more.

It was not just a store, it was an adventure. It was a treasure hunt, and a shopper's ark. There were two of everything. One did not go there only to shop, but to be entertained, enthralled, delighted, and surprised.

To step into that old log-and-frame two-story building (erected, some say, in 1910) was to be met by the pungent smells of tanned and untanned hides, oiled guns and tobacco. The wooden shelves — lining every wall — rose precariously to the ceiling and were stuffed with every sort of bric-a-brac imaginable. There were boxes upon boxes on the shelves upon shelves which contained not what the label indicated but some totally alien item. No one but Charlie knew where anything was — sometimes even Charlie was baffled — but that was part of the store's charm.

If ever there was a business run contrary to standard merchandising procedures, it was Charlie Main's. He violated every rule, and his customers loved it. And what's more, he made money in his off-handed way. He was an individualist, this gentle man who had found his way to Nome in 1904. He was a stocky man of medium height, who dressed casually in trousers and dark shirts. During the nearly fifty years he lived in Alaska, he was a trapper, trader, freighter and storekeeper.

His mixed bag of merchandise was a conglomerate he picked up when other stores went out of business; he was an indiscriminate buyer with the tendencies of a squirrel and the instincts of a pack rat. He stuffed goods into every nook and cranny until the shelves swayed and the walls bulged.

This crazy, mixed-up store was more or less taken for granted by the old-time residents who, whenever they needed a particular item, would say: "Charlie Main has it." It was the city slickers, arriving fresh from the East, who were dazzled by the unique style of the storekeeper, and one of them wrote about Charlie in a national magazine —*Mademoiselle,* no less — during World War II.

Consider this: When metal hairpins had vanished from the face of the earth during the 1940s, Charlie Main had them, and nylon stockings, too.

There were surprises at every turn — here an oil painting by Pete Johnson, one of Fairbanks' first artists, and there a black-snake whip. Here a pair of Cossack boots trimmed with mink, and there a stack of white enameled tin plates; here a muskrat hat, and there a tuxedo; here a mouth organ, and there a dog harness. There was stuff people didn't need, or even know existed.

At one time a little German lady, Miss Erheart, worked as Charlie's clerk. She was a tiny, fastidious person with wispy blonde hair and a strong accent. One day Miss Erheart was assisting a man who wanted a pair of eyeglasses (oh, yes, Charlie sold those, too). Miss Erheart took each pair of glasses from the tray, blew on the lenses, polished them with her handkerchief, and handed them to the customer.

"These are just about right," the man said, "but I would like them a little bit stronger."

Each lens had a number — 2, 4, 6, 8, etcetera — indicating the strength of the glasses. At this point Miss Erheart became confused. She did not know whether the large numbers or the small numbers were stronger.

Near the counter was a trap door in the floor which gave access to a cribbed basement where Charlie was working that particular day. Miss Erheart walked to the trap door and called down, "Mr. Main, on these eyeglasses, which is stronger, the 6s or the 8s?"

A booming voice resounded from the depths: "Sell him 8s, we got more of 'em."

That was Charlie Main.

Unfortunately, we will never have the opportunity to visit such a place again, not with the slide-rule boys designing store space, the computer tracking our buying habits, and our own demand for super-fast service.

In 1967, when the great flood of the century swept through here, Charlie Main's basement caved in and the building tipped at a dangerous angle. The structure was condemned as a safety hazard and slated for destruction.

A nostalgic few wanted to save the building and move it to another location, but that was too expensive, and the store probably would not have survived the uprooting anyhow. The day dawned when the old landmark with its rickety front steps and cracked windows was razed in a controlled burn; the ashes were plowed under by a bulldozer.

Goodbye, Charlie Main's.

That happened long after Charlie left the country in 1950 with his wife, Carol, to retire on Camano Island near Seattle. There he lived in comfort for five years until his passing at seventy-four.

No one has come along to take his place.

DREAM HOUSE

There is a house on the corner of Fifth and Cowles known as the Mary Lee Davis house, although it has been fifty years since she lived in it. According to the plaque on the side of the two-story frame dwelling, it was built in 1906. It stands today strong and sturdy, a monument to high-quality materials and workmanship, one of the few antique houses in Fairbanks worthy of preservation.

It is a house with an intriguing history. A Dawson miner married a beautiful young woman who wanted the best things in life, and that included living in San Francisco. But the husband — for reasons of his own — did not care to leave the North. He proposed a compromise: If she would live in Alaska ten years, he would build her the finest house in the whole darn Territory.

She took him up on the offer, but — for reasons of her own — she went to a lawyer and drew the plans and specifications for her dream house.

First and foremost, it was to have a real lawn; it must have a real fireplace; it must have hot water heat (her husband had to import a man from Seattle to install it); it must have oak floors, oak trim and doors; a large screened porch; a double garage and the best plumbing, with porcelain fixtures.

The contract specified a warm house, not a chinked log cabin with drafty floors, but one frame house set inside another, complete with six full inches of sawdust between the walls and ceiling to make it frost-proof in the winter and heat-proof in the summer.

The "finest house in the whole darn Territory," built for another woman, was to become known as the Mary Lee Davis House.

This little lady knew what she wanted. Her husband-to-be signed on the dotted line, and the house was built per specs. Unfortunately, not long after that the man died, leaving his wife with a house she could no longer afford, in a place where she no longer wished to be. The house changed hands many times, until the woman came along who made it famous.

Mary Lee and Allen Davis were from "back East" with ties in Boston and New York. His job was to established a U.S. Bureau of Mines in Alaska in the early 1920s. That took him to remote areas in the Territory, and on many of those trips he was accompanied by his wife, who recorded her observations in articles she wrote for *The Atlantic Monthly,* the *North American Review,* and *Scribner's,* and in her books, *We Are Alaskans* and *Uncle Sam's Attic.*

When the Davises first arrived in Fairbanks they rented a cabin — forty dollars a month — which never had a lock on the front door, near the library where Mary Lee was the director. Two years later they began house-hunting. Their quest led them to Fifth and Cowles.

Mary Lee wrote "We snatched upon this house as heaven-sent, and bought the place even though we could ill afford to." She described her home as ". . . a charming cottage, gray-painted, green-roofed, with a wide, spacious porch, window boxes of bright blossoms and hanging baskets with flowering vines. . . . The house was set back restfully from the street in a lawn of smooth-clipped grass that was our particular pride, for lawns were a true luxury and a daring experiment in this land of moss and under-frozen soil."

In her book, *Uncle Sam's Attic,* Mary Lee sings praises of her house with its built-in vacuum cleaner that sucked all the dust into a fireproof bin in the cellar. There was — even at that early date — "every electrical device we could have to make our living less complicated." In the basement, where the coal furnace was located, was a darkroom for developing, printing, and enlarging pictures.

The Davises built "the first open fireplace in our part of the country and a curiosity to many. On either side of the fireplace and topped by one slab of oak that stretched across the whole room, we built open oak bookcases and filled them with treasures."

They furnished the house with a grandfather clock, an old Nantucket desk, her great-grandmother's four-poster bed, and oriental rugs. On the open veranda was white wicker furniture for the lemonade-sipping days of summer.

Mary Lee wrote, "I will not tell of Alaska as one who went there as a tourist; nor did I make the trip to Alaska to gather information for a book. I lived there eight years in the heart of it. It was our home, our much loved home; and I have never called a place home with such zest and love as I have for Uncle Sam's Attic."

A number of years ago a young couple, Randal and Debbie Wallace, bought the Mary Lee Davis home and began restoring the golden oak of the door casings and the pillars and fireplace mantle that had been painted over by former residents, and preserving the beauty and original design of the structure. They maintained the high ceilings and wide windows with deep oak casings. They began furnishing the rooms with antiques. In the living room are a one-hundred-year-old, square Steinway piano and a glass-fronted china cabinet. Beneath the crystal chandelier in the dining room is an oak table with seven leaves and fourteen high-backed chairs.

There have been many changes since the house was built, but on the lawn the green grass flourishes, and in the downstairs bathroom the porcelain fixtures the first lady of the house requested are still in use.

SWINGING BRIDGE

Over Noyes Slough, where the green willows grew in summer and a black raven often sat on the tall pilings, was the old swinging bridge.

It was a spider-weblike construction of wire mesh and rope, wrapped around cables and poles strung across the slough at Slater Street. The bridge gave people in Graehl easy access to Slaterville, or vice versa, as you please.

The minute you set foot on this spineless wonder, it sprang to life like an aroused animal — bucking and lurching and setting the ropes a-tremble. It took courage to cross this mere nothing of a bridge, especially when the other side was a heart-thundering one hundred twenty-five feet away. A passing breeze could set the bridge in motion, and with any wind at all you were really flying high.

There were some — mostly boys — who dared ride their bikes across, clattering and rattling over the slats while the muddy slough winked its evil eye below. The planks had gaps between them where a shoe, or bare foot, could very easily get caught — oh, perish the thought! If by awful chance someone should start from the other

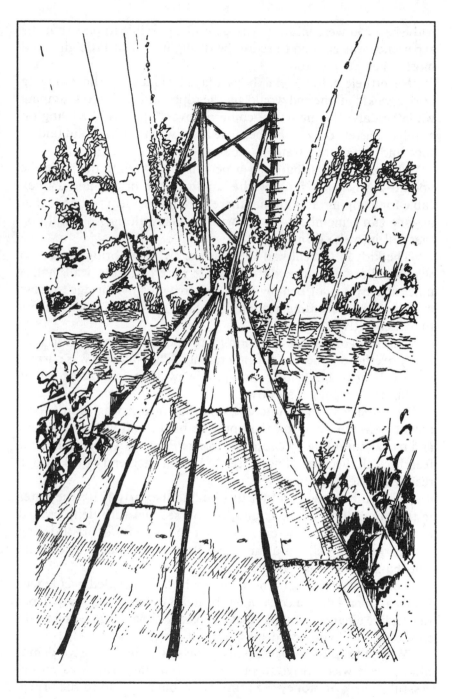

Set foot on this spineless wonder and it sprang to life like an aroused animal. Even a passing breeze could set it in motion.

end when you were midway across, it was possible to pass, but the experience was enough to scare the daylights out of little girls and most other people, too.

Nevertheless, daredevil boys played games on the swinging bridge. A kid at one end would get the ropes and cables to thumping while he dared his mate to "come on over." It was like being on a roller coaster, only worse because there was nothing solid underfoot and the murky water lay below.

The only things that kept a person from falling off were the up-and-down ropes running the length of the bridge and a thick cable for gripping. For all that there were no accidents — none that anyone can remember — well, with the exception of a small dog that fell into the drink.

The kids in Graehl had to cross the swinging bridge to get to school. Those who lacked the courage were forced to walk half a mile extra by way of Bentley Dairy. There was still a bridge to cross and there was no getting around this one; it was the only way across the Chena River.

This bridge was massive, intimidating, of steel construction with heavy overhead girders and sturdy railings. The walkway was narrow and the boards, laid end-to-end, gave view of the menacing roll of the big river a long way down.

The best way to handle crossing that bridge was: don't look down, keep your eyes on the opposite bank, and walk fast. Cars and trucks rumbling by caused a strong vibration which you could feel through the soles of your feet. A sign at each end of the bridge read: "Please walk horses."

When the swinging bridge was built in the early 1930s the water in the slough flowed freely and, of course, that turbulence added to the excitement of the crossing. But today, with debris littering the narrow channel, it is a sluggish waterway populated by beavers who have helped to stay the flow.

For twenty-five years the swinging bridge provided excitement for a summer's day, a convenient route to town, and a scary experience, like a haunted house, that tempted you back again and again to see whether you could master your fear.

When the Alaska Road Commission slated the bridge for demolition, there was a drive to preserve it, but the effort was unsuccessful — lack of money the primary problem — and so the bridge came down.

It was replaced in 1950 by a concrete bridge. All that remains of the landmark is memories and these few anonymous lines of poetry found in an abandoned cabin:

O Swinging Bridge, in future year,
When time has struck his blow,
And all who swung o'er thee when young,
Sleep in the mold below —
These lines perhaps may witness bear,
That once you stood in beauty there!
Let scoffers know it, that a poet —
Paid tribute with a tear!

WAECHTER BROS.

Time was when the name of Paul Manzel was a household word in Fairbanks. He was the butcher for Waechter Brothers' meat market on Second Avenue.

The one-story frame building had a false front to hide the pitched roof. The name "Waechter Bros." was painted in big letters across the top and could be seen from quite a distance. Large plate-glass windows on either side of the double doors sat almost as low as the wooden sidewalk. Striped canvas awnings that shaded the windows could be rolled back on cloudy days.

The air inside the market was decidedly cool and heavy with a peculiar odor, no doubt caused by the sides of beef, whole pigs, lambs and reindeer carcasses hanging on heavy hooks from the stout ceiling beams. The huge chunks of meat were brought out of cold storage and allowed to thaw before the butchers began cutting. They stood at the sturdy butcher's blocks in their blood-spattered aprons, using hand saws, heavy cleavers and long, gleaming knives.

In the glass case were white enamel trays full of German sausages and cuts of beef and pork. Most customers preferred to have their meat cut by Menzel. He wore a long white coat with white sleeve shields, a white shirt, white apron and black tie.

"Take your thumb off the scale, Paul," the customers joked as he weighed the meat on the big brass scale. He wrapped the meat in heavy white paper and bound it with string from a large spool hung high overhead. The ceiling and upper walls were covered with pressed tin in an intricate design, and painted white, contrasting with the dark wainscoting on the rest of the walls. Black and white

Paul Manzel was everyone's favorite butcher at Waechter Bros.,
which dominated the meat business for more than forty years.

floor tiles in a geometric design gave the shop a look of order and distinction in spite of the bloody chopping block. Light came from the milky-white glass fixtures suspended on chains from the ceiling.

It was a friendly meat market where young customers, picking up orders for their mothers, were given free dill pickles from the barrel. Soup bones were for the asking. So was liver for the cat.

"No people, no place have better meats, or a wider menu of fresh meats and game, from birds to reindeer to mountain sheep and big game . . . than have the contented residents of the 'Friendly North,' " said a Waechter Brothers' advertisement in an early Fairbanks magazine.

Waechter Brothers, established in Fairbanks in 1903, was owned by Henry and Ollie Waechter, who ran the operation from Seattle. During the gold rush of 1898 they set up a meat market in Dawson with outlets in Nome, Fairbanks, Nenana and Iditarod.

"No market is more up to date that ours," a Waechter ad stated. "We buy only the choicest meats, buy in great quantities in the states, ship north and cold storage by wholesale and sell locally at lower prices than the same meats bring in cities in the states." That kind of competition was pretty hard to beat.

Waechters dominated the meat business in Fairbanks for more than forty years.

In looking back — way back — we see that meat-marketing in Alaska got started under the hand of Henry and Ollie's father, William Waechter. He was the first man to bring cattle on the hoof to Dawson by way of Seattle. That meant wintering at Lake Bennett to build rafts, and then barging downriver when the Yukon River was free of ice.

William was an indomitable German who pushed north with his wife, his sons and his daughters on a cattle drive to Alaska by way of the Yukon to Circle City and overland to Fairbanks. The trip from Circle, a rugged hundred and sixty miles, was tough going and took its toll on man and beast.

William's sons operated Waechters from Seattle, but their sister Minnie stayed in Alaska and worked at the family store in Iditarod. There she married miner J.L. Brewis. They had three children, Gladys, Barbara and Henry. Henry lives in Delta Junction. The two girls, Gladys Sams, born in Iditarod, and Barbara Lindberg, born in Flat, have lived in Fairbanks since their parents took them there nearly six decades ago.

That is how history is made.

NORTHERN LIGHT LAGER

Nearly seventy years ago a fine brewery, owned by Herman Barthel, stood on the corner of First and Clay. The main building measured forty by seventy feet and stood four stories high to accommodate the huge brewing vats. There were two deep and

Barthel Brewery at First and Clay slaked Fairbanks thirst with Northern Light Lager until prohibition forced its closure.

commodious cellars where the beer was stored, a brewhouse forty by twenty feet with two storerooms on top, and a somewhat smaller engine room which housed the forty-five-horsepower engine.

It took two-hundred-fifty cords of split birch or spruce each year to keep the plant going. Radiators throughout the building guaranteed a steady temperature, so in summer it was not too hot, nor in winter too cool, an important factor in beer-making, or so we're told.

Somewhere under the Clay Street neighborhood are the remains of the Barthel ice house, built six feet under, capable of holding three hundred tons of Chena River ice.

The brewery could store many, many tons of goods. They had to have some place to put those three thousand beer kegs and fifteen thousand beer bottles waiting to be filled.

Speaking of beer kegs, the late Pop Wehner worked at the Barthel Brewery as a cooper, a maker of beer kegs. He used oak staves caulked with cattail reeds.

When it comes to beer — as any good brewmaster knows — it's the water that makes it good. Barthel's wells were sunk sixty feet deep. The water was pure, the supply unlimited. The product was called Northern Light Lager. A vast quantity of hops and malt was used, shipped in by the riverboats from California and Oregon.

The brewhouse had a capacity of one hundred barrels daily — enough to give each resident in town one bottle of beer a day, so said Herman Barthel in the April 3, 1910, issue of the *Fairbanks Times*. Adjacent to the beer plant was a small building where soft drinks in such flavors as strawberry and root beer were bottled.

By 1910 Barthel's could hold its own in terms of equipment and production with breweries in cities ten times its size in the States. Northern Light Lager, because of the excellent water and the know-how of the German brewmasters, was preferred by a great many people to the beer shipped in from Outside.

Herman Barthel, a Prussian by birth, had brewed beer for forty years before coming to Fairbanks. He engaged as his foreman one Rhinehart Effinger, a man who also had learned his trade in the Old Country.

According to the *Fairbanks Times* quoted earlier, "Given a population of about one hundred Americans and at least one German, it is a safe bet that a brewery site will be among the locations filed on the townsite plat, provided there is . . . more than enough water than is absolutely necessary for washing purposes."

Fairbanks had more than one hundred Americans, more than one German, more than enough water, and two breweries in 1910 — the other being the Arctic Brewery which Barthel later purchased.

In later years the Pioneer Brewery was doing business in a dark hulk of a building on the north bank of the Chena River, across from the Masonic Temple. Midnight Sun beer went down easy, and did a brisk business in the mid-1930s after prohibition.

While we are on the subject of prohibition, it was that piece of legislation in 1919 that put the Barthel Brewery out of business.

A certain Fairbanks resident — a teenager at the time — remembers well the day the marshals closed Barthels Brewery. All the kegs and huge vats of Northern Light Lager were dumped into a long sluice box that emptied into the Chena River. Men and boys stood shoulder to shoulder on both sides of the sluice box with mugs in both hands, drinking from that flowing river of beer as fast as they could chug-a-lug.

MILLER HOUSE

It seems a shame that Miller House, near Mile 114.5 on the Steese Highway, is gone without a trace — even the ashes of the historic landmark, burned in 1971, have been scattered on the wind.

The oldest roadhouse in Alaska, in continuous use from 1896, it was built by Fritz Miller and Casper Ellingen to accommodate the Birch Creek diggings, which were "struck" even before Dawson. Millions of dollars worth of gold came out of the ground — first by hand, then by dredge.

All that remains of Miller House is the memory of a sprawling log structure with its satellite cabins huddled in the dark, narrow valley among the rustling willows and the tailing piles. To look down the steep side road that plunges off the highway to that one-time center of warmth and cheer is to think of Frank and Graziella Miller, who kept the fires burning for more than thirty-three years. They provided room and board to travelers, sold groceries and gasoline to miners, and were postmasters from 1936 until the end.

There is memory, too, of the flag pole with the American and Alaskan flags flying smartly in the breeze that blows more often than not at that two-thousand-foot elevation. Everyone around those parts knew, of course, that the flags signified a post office. At its peak, two hundred miners got their mail at Miller House. Deliv-

Graziella Miller grew up in elite French boarding schools to become the gracious through hard-working hostess of Miller House.

eries in the early days came once a week by dog team, later by bush plane.

Mrs. Miller — Graziella, if you were on a first-name basis — was lively and energetic, a little lady in a hurry. She talked fast too, and never lost her French accent. Her touch was seen in the jungle of green plants in the windowsills, and in the beds of nasturtiums and bachelor buttons brightening the wooden sidewalks. Lack of modern conveniences never prevented her linen from being snowy white, her floors from being immaculate, and dinner from being on time.

It wasn't as if Grazeilla was born to lead such a life; far from it. She was born in France, where her father was an officer in the navy. He spoke nine languages. When Graziella was very young her mother died, leaving her to be reared by an aunt. Her early girl-hood was spent in boarding schools.

"When I was fifteen I decided I wasn't going to stay in school any more," said Graziella in a taped interview in 1969. "I was very spoiled."

Her father, who was in the hotel business in San Francisco, sent her five hundred dollars and a ticket to America. The year was 1905.

Some time later Graziella was married in San Francisco. In a tragic series of events, both her husband and her father died within a month of each other. She faced the challenge of supporting herself. "I had never worked a day in my life," she said. She went to beauty school in San Francisco and received a license to practice as a beautician and cosmetologist in 1910. She was twenty.

Why she chose to come to the North is not known, but it is known that she met Frank Miller in Livengood in 1915. He was the U.S. marshal. They married nine years later in Fairbanks. Frank's mining partner ran off when there were bills to pay, so Frank would not marry until he was out of debt.

Frank was a tall, slender gentleman from Kentucky. He arrived in Dawson in 1899 and took part in the stampedes in Circle, Fair-banks, Tolovana, Rampart and Livengood. Frank was not related to Fritz Miller, one of the roadhouse founders.

While operating Miller House, Frank maintained the old road-house custom that guests were not to carry in firewood or water, a tradition he honored well into his ninetieth year. He mastered the art of a quick fire by having on hand a few pieces of kindling and a spoonful of spruce sawdust mixed with coal oil. The drum stove in the store post office took three-foot lengths of wood and the heat it gave off was sufficient to keep people and plants happy even on the coldest day.

For many years travelers stopping at the roadhouse had dinner family-style at the long dining table that seated twelve in high-backed chairs. The lamps burned propane. On the walls were oil paintings by Ted Lambert and framed family pictures, and on the floor were

Miller House, built in 1896 to serve the Birch Creek diggings, operated for seventy-five years. Even its ashes are now gone.

wolf, lynx and fox skins. A set of classics in fancy bindings lined the bookshelf.

Against one wall was a pump organ of dark mahogany with a high back fitted with little shelves and mirrors and a place for a gas lamp, made by the Windsor Company of Chicago at the turn of the century, and brought in by a gold miner for his city-bred wife.

After Frank died in 1969, his wife remained at Miller House and chopped the wood and kept the place going until her death. After the roadhouse was sold (and before the fire), the contents were removed. Later they were offered for sale at public auction. Among the items offered were a wooden icebox, a solid bronze cash register, a freight wagon, a tuxedo, Frank's old rocking chair, and the pump organ.

It was late at night when the organ came up for bid. Interest was keen; the bidding was brisk. For some reason — no one knew why — a difference of opinion occurred between the auctioneer and a man in the crowd and the bidding stopped. Loud whispering ran through the room. During a long pause Mrs. Rosalie Abel held up her card, and without any further bidding the auctioneer said, "Sold!"

Later Rosalie said, "I had no intention of buying the organ. It was my first and only bid." The price was forty-four hundred dollars.

With the organ, which is still in good condition, were the family pictures Mrs. Miller kept on the mahogany shelves, and a shopping bag full of sheet music circa 1900. Some of the tunes were "The Kiss That Made Me Cry," "Let the Rest of the World Go By," and "Somebody's Waiting All Alone." They are songs Graziella played on the little organ very long ago at Miller House.

CREAMER'S DAIRY

The year is 1904. It is summer — July, to be exact — and two families, the Hinckleys and the Creamers, are among the passengers traveling by steamer up the Yukon and Tanana rivers to the new gold camp at Fairbanks.

The Hinckley party includes Charles, Belle, and her twenty-year-old sister, Annie Carr. On the cargo deck are Hinckley's horse and two cows. Hinckley sells milk to pay for the trip.

The family began the voyage at Nome, where they had lived several years and operated a dairy business. Annie worked at the Billy Rowe Boarding House and during her free time rode horseback on the beach.

The Creamer family includes Mary Jane Todd Creamer, her five daughters, and one son, Charlie Albert Creamer, born in Weaverville, California, in 1889. Mary is taking the children to join their father, Charles, who is operating a sawmill with his brother-in-law, Fred Noyes. Creamer also operates a ferry on the Chena River. In the winter he cuts ice for sale. He first came to Alaska in 1897 and spent a short time in Juneau before going to Dyea, where he freighted goods from the dock to Sheep Camp on the Chilkoot Trail.

Creamer had three teams of horses, and when he was short of help he put Charlie, who was only eight years old, in the driver's seat. Young Charlie's impressions of the raucous life in Dyea and Skagway, of the infamous Randolph "Soapy" Smith and of the multitudes crossing the Chilkoot, lasted a lifetime.

Annie Carr, who was baptized Anastacia Elizabeth, describes the trip from Nome in an autobiography she began but never completed: "The trip up the Yukon took three weeks. It was a beau-

Creamer's Dairy, run by the same family for sixty-two years, is now on the National Registry of Historic Places, and Creamer's field is now a state bird sanctuary.

tiful trip — nature all so green after the barren beaches of Nome. We had fresh vegetables and game picked up at trading posts where we stopped to get wood for the boat. At last Fairbanks! We were all so happy to get on land again. We cleared a place to build, and cut logs for a house and a barn at Fourth and Kellum."

The first winter in Fairbanks the Creamer family lived in a log cabin and the children attended school, until it ran out of money before the year was out. Young Charlie, fourteen at the time, was not much interested in book learning, so the closure suited him just fine. In the summer of 1905 he worked on a cattle drive from Circle to Fairbanks with Ralph Waechter. There were several slaughter houses and cold-storage businesses in town to supply the local meat markets. Charlie quit school and worked in Waechter Brothers' meat market for three years, cattle driving in summer and delivering meat in winter. His father built a two-story frame house on the north side of the Chena, near the Wendell Bridge.

Not long after the Hinckleys arrived in Fairbanks, they moved their dairy to the Graehl area. That same year Annie Carr married Louie Golden, a card parlor, saloon, and dance-hall entrepreneur. Annie did not approve of Louie's business, so persuaded him to sell it and buy a grocery store. Golden's Grocery was housed in a small frame building which later became Palfy's Sheet Metal Shop. It has been preserved at Alaskaland, a historical park in Fairbanks.

In the meantime, Belle and Charles Hinckley expanded their dairy business. In 1913 they purchased the Murray homestead and located the dairy on the three hundred acres of pastureland on the north side of town.

Annie and Louie were doing well in their business, but not in their marriage. Annie made frequent trips to Tacoma to visit her mother, traveling by stage to Valdez and by boat to Seattle.

Young Charlie Creamer continued to live in Graehl with his father. He worked as a pin-setter at the bowling alley, bartender at the California Saloon, and on a road crew constructing the Chena Hot Springs road. He was a tall, handsome young man, and a favorite with the ladies.

Charlie enlisted in the Army in World War I, and got as far east as Iowa before the war ended and he was discharged. He returned to Fairbanks in 1918 and got a job working on the Alaska Railroad. About that time, Annie and Louie Golden were divorced. The grocery store was sold and Louie left Alaska.

Two years later Charlie and Annie were married in Washington State. They operated a chicken farm at Pioneer, Washington, near Vancouver, and in 1922 their son, Donald, was born. The couple had a great love for Alaska and were happy to return, in 1927, to visit the Hinckleys and deliver livestock to Charlie's father in Fairbanks.

When Charlie learned that the Hinckleys wanted to sell the dairy, he auctioned his holdings in Washington, borrowed six thousand dollars from Fairbanks merchant Billy McGrath, and bought them out. The farm consisted of a log barn, a small log house, and a few sheds. Milk was delivered by horse and wagon.

In 1938 Charlie built a modern barn of Gothic proportions, thirty-six by one hundred and ten feet, which he painted white and trimmed in black. That imposing structure still stands as the focal point in the group of farm buildings — all painted white with black trim — that comprise Creamer's Dairy. It is the only group of pioneer farm buildings still standing in the Interior. Included is the original two-story farmhouse where Annie and Charlie lived, the bunkhouse, and the boiler house where wood (and later coal) generated heat for all the buildings. The dairy was operated by members of one family from 1904 until it closed in 1966.

At the peak of operation there were eight hundred acres in cultivation and pasture and more than one hundred milk-producing cows. Annie and Charlie installed milk- and ice-cream processing equipment and owned a fleet of modern delivery trucks. They sold livestock and poultry feed and raised and sold tons of potatoes. Milk was twenty-five cents a quart.

Because of the severe climate, the cows were kept in the big barn from October through April. The accumulation of manure was spread twice daily over the fields. Charlie spent many cold hours on the manure spreader.

In the spring, when the sun had melted the snow and pools of water lay over the open fields, the migrating ducks and geese made Creamer's field an annual stopover on their flight to northern nesting grounds. The seeds and grains in the manure fed the hungry birds, which arrived daily in mid-April in great flocks, squawking and calling. In a short time Charlie could identify the many species of waterfowl. "Charlie's birds" still find repast in those same fields which today are a bird sanctuary established by the State of Alaska.

A few months after Annie's death in 1966, Charlie closed the dairy which had provided Fairbanks with fresh milk for more than sixty years. Creamer had outlasted his competitors by working seven days a week for thirty-eight years, without a vacation. Several years later the property was sold, but it was no longer operated as a dairy.

In 1975 Creamer's Dairy was included in the National Register of Historic Places. The other landmarks so designated in Fairbanks are: the Immaculate Conception Church, George C. Thomas Memorial Library, the U.S. Post Office and Court House, and the riverboat *Nenana*.

Scenes From Childhood

Arnold Wold came from Duluth in 1926. His daughters (left to right), Kay, Bonnie and Jo Anne, were born in Fairbanks.

Scenes From Childhood

HOUSE ON FIRST AVENUE

Our house was, architecturally speaking, an Alaskan Shotgun design, sometimes known as an add-on. Originally it was a log cabin that telescoped, by virtue of frame additions, into a long, narrow structure incorporating living room, hallway, bedroom, bathroom and kitchen as it went along.

Six of the nine houses on the block were log look-alikes, with the same pitched tin roof, generous overhang and large front window. They, too, had grown at a whim, expanding as the family got bigger and the money came along.

Our house was set back from the street allowing a spread for a lawn. We could not afford that so the space was used for growing potatoes and cabbages. As my sisters and I grew older we noticed that other people didn't raise vegetables in their front yards, so we took the notion that we shouldn't either. We persuaded Mother to spend her money on lawn seed, with the promise that we would tend the grass.

We had no idea what we were getting in for. There was no outdoor water spigot so we had to carry water from inside the house; we had no lawn mower so we had to borrow one from the neighbors, and we were ignorant in the ways of weeding and feeding, so we got a lawn of malnourished grass and a thriving crop of dandelions and foxtails. Presiding over this disreputable patch of green was a tall, shaggy cottonwood tree which, when it wasn't dropping sticky pods, littered the grass with cotton tufts.

We were consoled by the fact that there wasn't a decent lawn on the entire block. But flowers — now that was another thing. Next door, Mrs. Huebner strung up lines to the cabin eaves for the sweet peas to climb, and climb they did in the long sun-drenched days of summer. The Manvilles had sweet peas too, down the entire length of their driveway and bordering the street, hanging on a wire fence that seemed ten feet tall to me at the time.

But in those days it was the inside of the house that was important, not the outside. My father, who earned ninety cents an hour as a mechanic at the Fairbanks Exploration Company, bought our house on First Avenue, along the river front, in 1946, for two thousand dollars. "It needed lots of fixing up," was the way Mother described it.

They began remodeling by turning the kitchen into a bathroom and the storeroom into a kitchen. The indoor plumbing eliminated the need for the sloped-roof one-holer out back, but the outhouse remained for many years after its retirement. The kitchen, now in the frame addition, had two sunny windows and a long counter with lots of cupboards, both upper and lower. There were deep bins — two of them — which held one-hundred-pound sacks of flour or sugar.

The stove was an oil-fired cooking range with a black top, which Mother used for a griddle when she cooked pancakes on Sunday morning. She kept a high polish on that stove by scrubbing it with a grill brick and waxing it with a candle. Heat from the range warmed water in a large tank in the bathroom.

The big bedroom, which belonged to my sisters and me, was also in the frame addition, originally the garage. The garage doors at the end of the room were boarded over on the inside, leaving just one windowpane uncovered. From the outside the big doors were plainly visible. The room also had a long window on one side which opened from the top and tipped back into the room, letting in light and air. In the winter, when the window was sealed shut, fresh air came from what we called the porthole — an opening in the wall near the ceiling. That was our air-conditioning, regulated by plugging or unplugging the hole with a wad of fabric.

In the corner of the bedroom sat the wood stove. It not only kept us warm, but the heat also dried the laundry strung on lines across the ceiling. My sisters and I would lie in bed and look up at wet sheets and underwear and breathe deeply of damp wool and Fels Neptha [soap]. After we went modern with a hand-fed stoker in the basement, the clothes were dried on racks over the registers.

Our house had other idiocyncrasies. There was a hallway between the living room and the kitchen which had six doors in the space of fifteen feet! There was a doorway at each end, of course, plus one each to the bedroom, the bathroom and the pantry, and a trap door in the floor to the cribbed basement. Naturally when the trap door was open there was a large hole in the floor. Since the hallway was a well-traveled thoroughfare, with people popping in or out of one door or another, extreme caution had to be taken when the trap door was up. We had some close calls, but no disasters.

There was one other oddly placed opening — a large square cut in the middle of the kitchen ceiling. A heavy plywood cover, painted the same color as the ceiling, fit snugly over the hole.

"What is that?" visitors asked.

"The attic."

"How do you get up there?"

That was not so easy to explain. We moved the sewing table under the opening and stood on it, reached up and pushed the plywood cover into the attic far enough that someone could be hoisted through the hole.

Once you were in the attic your troubles were not over. One misstep between the beams, and you would go through the Celotex ceiling into the kitchen. While watching your feet you forgot about your head, and cracked it on the rafters. Coming down took some courage too, and trust that the person on the sewing table would grab you as you dropped from on high.

There were wonderful treasures in the attic — an old rocking chair, Mother's trunk from Duluth, an old table that "came over with the Russians," boxes of Christmas decorations, and a great lot of junk we never would have missed if it had simply disappeared. But that jumble of useless odds and ends was kept safe during the Great Flood of 1967, while four feet of water swamped the house, ruining the rugs, chairs, tables, clothes, books and bedding.

Most everything on the main floor was damaged with the exception of the pictures on the wall and Mother's sequined evening dress, which floated on a foam-rubber mattress for nearly a week. It was in mint condition, along with the Christmas decorations and the Easter baskets high and dry in the attic.

After the floodwaters receded and we surveyed the mess, it seemed impossible we would ever live in our house again. The basement had caved in at the back door and there was structural damage caused by shifting support posts. But the house was still standing, and there was no place else to go.

It was mid-August, winter was approaching, and not a single piece of equipment operated — not the furnace, the hot water heater, the stove, the refrigerator, the typewriter, the toaster nor the coffee pot. There was mud a foot thick on the floor, and the basement had water up to the top step.

Inch by inch we scoured our way back into the house and spent one last winter there. The cases of bleach, the cans of air freshener and the gallons of Pine Sol barely made a dent in the musty flood-smell that rose from the floors.

In 1968 the City of Fairbanks purchased our house and all the others on the block to make room for the expansion of the city utility system. At the last minute our cabin was saved from destruction by the Tanana Valley Historical Society, who moved the log part to Alaskaland, the city's historical park, where it stands today.

No matter that the house has departed the neighborhood; no matter that the people who once lived there are gone; no matter that the rooms are empty and the lights have gone out, the house lives intact in somebody's memory.

Daddy did not live to see all this happen, nor even to finish the remodeling he and Mother had planned. He became ill with leukemia, and died in 1948.

PLAYHOUSES

The playhouse of my earliest memory was the cubbyhole on the side of our house, where the frame addition jutted out from the original log cabin and formed an ell. In that ell my father had built a sturdy platform to cradle the fifty-gallon oil barrel which fed the small heater in the living room.

The oil stand, open on two sides, was about three feet off the ground. The underside of the barrel provided a roof over our heads, and the sides of the house became the walls of our hideaway. It was shady and cool, with the tall grass and willows providing greenery. My sisters and I took our dolls and toys out there and ate peanut-butter and jelly sandwiches. As we got older we began to find fault with our little nook. It was too small, it smelled oily, and there was no way we could fix up the underside of a barrel and stout posts. Our domestic instincts were being stifled; it was time to move on.

My uncle, who was in the storage and transfer business, had a warehouse a few blocks up the street. There he had the most wonderful collection of packing crates — huge affairs, big enough for my sisters and me to get inside and stand upright. Some of the boxes were of heavy cardboard framed with wood. Others were just cardboard, but of such a toughness that it resisted our efforts to cut windows with butcher knives.

The Wold house on First, of Alaskan add-on design, had an ell and a platform to hold the oil barrel and be a little girls' playhouse.

With Uncle Sig's permission my sister Kay and I took the crates home by turning them end over end — bam! bam! bam! — along the dirt street to our backyard. We set them up beyond the clothesline poles, hoping (in vain) that Mother would somehow overlook them.

One time we got too ambitious, stacked box on top of box, and made an apartment house. It was unsafe and it looked outrageous, especially when we covered it with a tarp. We furnished it with rugs and curtains from the ragbag and naturally thought it quite an attraction. No one else thought so. Mother especially was not impressed. "I want you to get rid of that mess out there," she said. We knew by her tone it was time to move again.

Very often we went to the Tonseths' house at the end of the block to play upstairs in Dorothy's room. The house had a steeply pitched roof, which made a high ceiling in the center of the room and low eaves on the sides. Dorothy's bed was under the eaves on one side, and on the other a wall had been built to provide storage space under the eaves. It extended the length of the room like a tunnel — a very dark tunnel.

We entered this hideaway through a small door — it reminded me of Alice going down the rabbit hole. The door had a handle on the outside only. If we closed it from the inside, there was no way to open it. When that happened — and it did, more than once — we had to bang on the floor until Dorothy's mother came to see what the fuss was all about.

We went into the hideaway on our hands and knees — it was impossible to stand up without banging our heads on the rafters — dragging with us a small lamp on an extension cord, the doll house, and our dolls. There we whiled away the hours during the days of childhood when time was no concern.

For all the joys of our attic retreat, our favorite haunt was Tonseths' old garage. The car, stored there all winter, was parked more conveniently in the street during the summer, leaving the garage open to squatters.

It was a log structure, originally a pioneer cabin — the typical type with moss roof and chinking, built close to the ground to conserve heat. It had two rather nice windows, minus glass, one on either side. Two large doors opened at one end to allow the car to enter.

Our playhouse was furnished with a single iron cot — no mattress, just the springs — a large, dusty rolltop desk, a dead battery, two tires, and a pair of sheep horns mounted on the wall.

The ceiling was covered with heavy cheesecloth, called a balloon ceiling in its day — and over the years the cheesecloth had collected a heavy loak of dust. My sisters, Dorothy and I loved to get brooms and beat the dust out of the cheesecloth until we fell into a coughing fit. Once the dust settled we got busy and swept the floor until we had another whirlwind stirred up. All that dirt seemed to satisfy our sense of housekeeping as no job at home had ever done. Here was a floor that really needed sweeping.

To add to its charm, the garage was banked by raspberry bushes. Some could be picked by lying on the bedsprings and leaning out the window. And then Mrs. Tonseth was kind enough to plant her vegetable garden between the garage and the house, inviting numerous raids on tender peas and new carrots.

The garage was our fort, our castle, our barn, our tepee, and our little house in the woods. We outfitted it with banana crates and Blazo boxes that served us well as cupboards, tables and chairs. One summer we began cooking out there. Of course, we never asked whether it was "all right" — we just did it.

The stove was a simple affair made of a large coffee can with a grate on top and a Sterno candle for fuel. It was possible, with a little bit of luck, to heat tomato soup and grill cheese sandwiches on the stove. It was also possible to burn down the garage, but we never did.

The destruction of the garage came about in a less dramatic way. During the 1967 flood the Chena River came rolling down the block and caused all kinds of havoc. The houses and the old garage were left standing, but their days were numbered. A year later the city bought the block to make room for the power-plant expansion and the garage gave way to the future.

THE CATLOT

What makes a good neighborhood? From a kid's point of view it is measured in terms of places to play. Take the grassy meadow across the street from our house, where we played baseball; take the old river steamer sunk in the mud on the riverbank, where we roamed the decks; take the river ice, where we went skating. Take the marshes, where we stalked cattails beyond the range of Mother's voice. Now, that was a good neighborhood.

There was no manicured park, no gym set, not even a yard with slides and swings. Our playground was wherever we decided to play. Sometimes it was in the middle of the dirt street, where games of kick-the-can, Mother may I and hide-and-seek attracted fifteen kids and more.

We roller-skated on the sidewalk in front of our house. We played hopscotch and jumped rope. We sold Kool Ade from a card table under the cottonwood tree.

But the thing that made our neighborhood better than all the others in town was the Catlot. The Catlot was the property of the Northern Commercial Company, a street-to-street corner lot at Second and Cleary, bordered by Torgerson's greenhouse.

The Catlot was a storage yard for old Caterpillar tracks — hence the name — and huge spools of wire. There were piles of telephone poles and old tires. There were big motors and lengths of chain. There was a warehouse on the property, a long, windowless building, its unpainted siding blackened with age. The building was padlocked, but there was an attic opening where some of the boys managed to break in.

There were never any acts of vandalism at the Catlot that I recall. It was never fenced nor posted "No Trespassing." Our parents never put it off-limits. A few panes of Torgerson's greenhouse were broken during the years, but not by deliberate act on our part.

Oh, the games of hide-and-seek that went on there! Think of the centers of the coiled Cat tracks, perfect places to hide. Think of the pile of telephone poles, pungent with the scent of creosote, as a mountain to be climbed, or a fort to be defended. Come to think of it, it probably wasn't a very safe place to play. Every nook and cranny, by today's standards, would be considered hazardous to our health, but such things were not considered when I was ten years old.

When we tired of Cat tracks, telephone poles, tall grass and the warehouse, we were ready for the old stagecoach. It wasn't much to look at — the years had taken their toll — but it was still intact with wooden wheels, leather rigging and a place to sit, even if it was a wood plank. The stage was very heavy and impossible to move, but with considerable effort we could get it to rock back and forth, and with a lot of imagination we could see the backs of the horses pulling us over the old Valdez-Fairbanks Trail. We could hear the clip-clopping of the horses' hooves. We could hear the crack of the whip and the rush of the wind. We climbed the mountains and ferried the rivers. The stagecoach was our time machine and the Catlot was our Disneyland.

Meet ya at the Catlot!

THE LAKE

In one way my childhood was deprived. We did not have a cabin at the lake. I do have memories of the lake, those special times we went to Auntie's cabin, or spent the weekend with the Tonseths, but it did not seem often enough and it was not like having a place of your own.

When I say Lake, I mean Harding — named in 1923 after a visit by President Harding — a forty-mile drive from town over the then-unpaved Richardson Highway. To have a cabin at The Lake was a mark of distinction, even in Fairbanks, where the residents prided themselves on a lack of social rank. The trip usually began early Saturday morning and took several hours over rocks and ruts, with clouds of dust blowing at us from the cars ahead.

As the car turned off the highway onto the country lane that twisted through the forest of leafy birch and spreading spruce, I sat up straighter to get first glimpse of the blue water. It was a large, lovely oval whose distant shore was usually mist-shrouded in the morning light. The trees, putting down roots in the rich soil nourished by underground springs, grew tall, straight and full with foliage. The underbrush was a lush spread of flat-leafed willows and wild roses. From the treetops I heard the peep and call of chickadees and sparrows.

Auntie's cabin was at the end of the road that circled halfway around the lake. We drove slowly to keep the dust down and to check the driveways to see who else had come out for the weekend. The cabins we passed were simple and unpretentious; some log, others frame construction, with windows overlooking the water. Each had a steep set of stairs down to the dock. There was no running water nor electricity, but that gave the cabins their charm — we were roughing it just like the pioneers. We too, had to hike to the outhouse, a foul-smelling shanty a few paces beyond the woodpile.

Auntie's cabin was of unpeeled log slabs set among tall spruce trees whose greenish-gray boughs cast deep shadows, and whose huge roots intertwined on top of the ground to trip little girls with bare feet. Hanging from the branches were baskets of trailing nasturtiums, and on the tree stumps were planters of pansies. The sloped tin roof of the cabin was painted Chinese red to match the window trim.

The walls inside were natural birch. The cabin had three rooms: the front room with its windows overlooking the water, the middle room with its fireplace and bed, and the back room with its gas stove, cupboards and sink which drained into a bucket. In the floor was a trap door which opened to reveal a shallow hole. That was Auntie's cooler where the perishables were kept, including the potato salad for which she was justly famous. No one made it better. She cut the potatoes, the little green onions, the celery and cucumbers into perfect sizes and blended them with hard-cooked eggs and a dressing tangy with wine vinegar and Coleman's mustard.

Most of the lake cabins were furnished with cast-offs from the town houses, so you could sit on the chairs in a wet bathing suit and no one gave a darn. I remember the beds at the Tonseths' cabin were iron cots with lumpy mattresses and rough sheets, and the quilts weighed a ton. The pure wool Army blankets were a terrible khaki green — but welcome on a chilly night.

Their cabin had two rooms — the kitchen and a bedroom like a dormitory, with all the beds (four of them) side by side. There we slept under heavy blankets — happy as clams — in the half light of a sub-Arctic summer night.

Auntie's furnishings were something else. She had an oak table with a drop-leaf where we took our meals and where we played cards within the glow of the kerosene lamp. In the middle room was a buffet of dark wood with narrow drawers and fancy knobs, and a mirrored-back bar. She had a china cabinet of fine quality, with glass doors and a shelf for fancy tea cups. On the wall was a tapestry of brightly painted fruits — very red, shiny apples and long yellow bananas — that someone had sent long ago from Mexico. On the front windowsill was a plastic bank — a pink pig standing upright, dressed in blue overalls with a red cap on his head. I have no idea where that came from.

My sisters and I gathered firewood, and made endless trips to the dock to dip pails of clear water for washing dishes. We bathed in the lake — it was fed by a spring — and washed our hair with shampoo that created acres of lather across the blue water. There were other tasks, too, sweeping and dusting, and washing the glass chimneys for the lamps, but the days seemed longer then and we still found time to paddle Auntie's canoe along the shoreline, or sit in the sun with a book.

My sisters and I were not very good swimmers, although we did our share of wading where the water was shallow and the lake floor smooth and sandy. When we graduated from dog-paddling to swimming, we struck out for the wooden platform anchored in deep water where the big kids sunned and docked their motorboats.

There were few motorboats on the lake in those days. The ones we remember were the ten-horsepower variety that purred across the water — no more bothersome than the horseflies buzzing in our ears. No one had a radio, much less television. The lake was so quiet we could hear the creak of an oar across the water and the rustle of the wind in the aspen trees.

Perhaps my childhood was not so deprived, after all.

ROOT BEER WEATHER

There was a time, come summer, when it was root-beer making weather. As kids we usually took on the task during those loose-end days when there was "nothing to do."

We went into production in the Tonseths' backyard. They lived in a two-story log house with an attached greenhouse. The board-walk, which separated the greenhouse from the garden plot, was where we assembled our equipment. Near at hand was the needed garden hose.

We used a large galvanized washtub for mixing the brew. As soon as the cap was off the Hires Root Beer extract bottle, the taste buds tingled. Ah, delicious. This deep mahogany-hued extract was poured over a huge mound of white sugar. Water was added from the garden hose until we had almost five gallons. Half a yeast cake, dissolved in warm water, was strained through a cheesecloth and added.

With a wooden paddle this good stuff was stirred until "well mixed." The bottles, collected during the winter, were an assort-ment of beer, pop and other containers — glass strong enough to withstand the pressure the yeasty brew would exert. No one liked the business of washing the bottles, but it had to be done so we all shared in the chore. Even though hot water for scrubbing was carried from the house, sanitation and sterilization did not have top priority on those beer-making days on the boardwalk. We did carry water from the house, and splash a lot of it around, but it did not always go where it was most needed.

When it came to filling the bottles with a cup and funnel, the job was messier yet. Now I learn that the youth of today put the tub on a table, insert a small hose, and siphon the beer into the bottles. No fuss, no muss, little bother.

At first everyone wanted to use the bottle capper. That meant center the bottle, hold the cap in place, pull the handle to fix the cap. After the novelty wore off, it became work, and took the better part of an afternoon.

When at last the brew was bottled, we lugged our treasure down the steep wooden steps to the Tonseths' basement, among the cobwebs and vegetable bins, where no sunlight nor draft strayed. There the bottles, placed carefully on their sides, lay to do their effervescent best.

The waiting began. Five days seemed an unbearable length of time. Some sampling took place before the fifth day, just to see how the drink was progressing. If by chance the storage area became too warm, the bottles would explode. Boom! Bam! Boom!

For some reason the very first bottle of root beer was the best — sweet and tingly, sliding down the throat smooth as satin with the little bubbles exploding flavor all the way to your stomach. By the time we were on our fourth or fifth bottle, we became more discriminating. "This one is a little flat," or, "It tastes kind of yeasty."

The true test of any batch was whether the beer, when first uncapped, would shoot over the top of the Tonseths' clothesline. Sometimes it did, sometimes it didn't, but fizzy or flat, we drank it just the same.

There was this chance, too: if we waited long enough the root beer would become beer — a somewhat foul-tasting concoction, but beer nonetheless.

Certain practices during my Fairbanks childhood — such as root-beer making — evolved from need. We did not have money to buy carbonated drinks, so we made our own. There was drama (how would it turn out?) and excitement (how many would blow their lids?) in our root-beer making business. Who, I wonder, will recall any sense of pleasure or accomplishment at putting coins in a pop machine and pulling the levers? Is that the way to nostalgia?

Even today root-beer making at home is one of the best buys around. The ingredients cost about two dollars, and when you figure you get fifty eight-ounce bottles, well, you get the feeling that it is root-beer making weather again.

SCHOOL DAYS

All my school years except one were spent in Fairbanks. When my sister Kay and I were very young we lived in a log house at the corner of Third and State, a house which is still standing, although it lists to the east and sinks deeper into the ground with each passing year. It was a mile to school along wooden sidewalks and across dirt streets.

The Fairbanks Public School was a massive square building of reinforced concrete, four stories high, as uninviting as a prison with its massive facade and gray paint. I started kindergarten in the basement and worked my way up, floor by floor.

There was neither color nor beauty in our classrooms, no relief from the drab-colored paint save the roll-down map of the world. The outside wall had tall windows with many panes, and dull shades to pull against the sun. The blackboards were black; the desks were of dark wood, the seats and writing tables all one unit, hitched together in straight, unyielding rows. We sat in those rows hour after hour, day after day, year after year.

The school was a maze of hallways and staircases. After the new addition was built and more stairways were added, it took what seemed like years to figure out how to get from floor to floor. The hallways, long and monotonously the same, were painted a grim, nondescript gray to absorb a decade of dirt and not need repainting. The deciding factor must have been, the drearier the color, the cheaper the paint, and precious little money was spent on that.

One winter we had a school bus, wonderfully welcome on very cold mornings, but in the afternoons when the sun was shining, I preferred to walk home and pocket the fifteen-cent fare. Mother, who was more interested in my safety than in my bankroll, squelched my scheme by insisting I give the money back if I didn't take the ride. I rode.

In the fall and late spring we walked. The morning was no time for slowpokes. If the gang passed your house and you weren't ready, they went on. There was, hanging over our heads, the threat of facing the principal, the stern Mrs. Pilgrim, if we were late. She was a cranky old woman and she looked the part, with dark hair

Classrooms were stark, discipline was stern, but learning was absorbed and memories are washed with a patina of pleasantness.

pulled back in a severe bun and a face without a smile. The kids said she kept a paddle in the office, and it wasn't just for show, either.

In those days you had to watch your step. Even minor infractions drew punishment. One time a fourth-grade boy was exiled to the hallway because he had garlic on his breath. How simple the world was then!

In kindergarten I was introduced to the delights of finger painting, and crowned the year by dancing around the maypole in a long dress with ribbons in my hair. Later I had a fling on stage as the Miller's Daughter in the grade school production of "Rumplestiltskin." One of my first literary efforts was a twelve-act play about Hiawatha, which I wrote when I was nine. Fortunately, not a single page has survived.

In the spring the high school students raised money for school events by staging a variety show called "Arctic Capers." It was the only live entertainment we had all year.

The school auditorium was packed with an adoring crowd of family, friends and grade-schoolers gazing with envy at the sophisticated antics of the upper-classmen. I dreamed of the day when I could sing "Shine on Harvest Moon" while some boy played the banjo and a crowd applauded.

In the fourth grade, with Miss Weller in charge, I advanced my reading skills, tackled geography and history, and had my first encounter with fractions. I practiced penmanship, rows and rows of circles to limber up the writing hand, and rows of lines up and down — push-pull, push-pull — across the tablet. A practice now taboo, I'm told, although I can't say it did me any harm.

Miss Weller, who shared her love of outdoor sports with us, involved the entire grade school in the ice-skating races held during the Winter Carnival. She spent hours of her own time teaching us the proper stance, timing us, and encouraging us to practice. "Practice makes perfect," she said, and we believed her.

We skated in the dark, we skated in the snow, we skated at thirty below zero. We skated to win, and we skated to be chosen for the drill team which performed during the Winter Carnival. If you were lucky enough to be on the team, you got to wear a red sweater and a navy-blue skirt. Those of us on the team imagined ourselves quite beautiful as we swept across the ice with our silver blades flashing — the new wave of Sonja Henies in Fairbanks.

Playground activities revolved around the seasons. In the spring we played jump rope and marbles; in the winter we played a kind of hockey game, with the teams kicking a tin can across the ice. Between seasons there were pom-pom-pull-away, king of the mountain, and tag.

In the fifth grade I was still carrying a sack lunch and envying the "big kids" who were free to go across the street to the Hi-Spot — a cafe in a small cabin — where they ate hamburgers, drank Coke, and played the juke box. Other girls wore brown loafers while my sister and I plodded along in lace-up oxfords. We waited, we wished and we longed to grow up.

My school memories have to do with sights and sounds, with game-playing, but very little about learning. I suppose I assimilated learning without too many traumas.

Those years are washed with a patina of pleasantness. I know in reality they could not have been all blissful, but if my strongest memories are happy, let me consider myself lucky. And if I failed to say thank you to the teachers who broadened and enriched my life, and who established my education on a firm foundation, let me say it now.

TURKEY TRADITION

Our Thanksgiving turkey did not come from the supermarket, showered and shaved and ready to push into the oven with some mass-produced concoction supposed to pass for stuffing — no indeed! And neither did it have a pop-up thermometer to tell when it was done. You knew it was done by a squeeze of the drumstick and a thing called know-how.

The bird, never less than twenty pounds, thawed on the sideboard overnight. In the morning Mother pulled the giblets and neck from the cavity and put them into a pot with onions to simmer gently until tender. This set the stage — aromatically speaking — for the star attraction. From the simmering pot came the first whiffs of, yes, t-u-r-k-e-y!

Big Tom was then deposited in the kitchen sink where Mother, armed with tweezers, a paring knife and pliers, attacked the tenacious pinfeathers lodged in the pimply white skin. She plucked steadfastly, and when she was done she bathed the turkey in baking soda to keep it fresh. The next step was to find room in the already overcrowded refrigerator. After much rearranging and a quick disposal of leftovers, the turkey was shoehorned onto a shelf until stuffing time.

With a great deal of rattling and banging in the cupboard, Mother finally located the food grinder, which was rarely in use from turkey to turkey. The grinder was attached to the end of the table with a screw clamp, and my sisters and I broke up the dry bread and odds and ends of rolls and poked them into the grinder. We took turns cranking the handle, but our arms tired long before the job was finished. At that point Mother took over and we watched as the crumbs rose up like snowy mountain peaks from the bottom of the black roasting pan.

When that was done Mother melted butter — nothing less than butter — in a large cast-iron skillet and sauteed chopped onions and celery. The simmering and sauteing sent powerful messages to our taste buds. We didn't think we could *wait* until the dinner was ready.

The giblets, which had been doing their stuff on top of the stove, were divided with half designated for the dressing and the other half for the gravy. We snapped up as many of the long, sweet pieces of neck meat as we could take without getting rapped on the knuckles with Mother's long-handled chopping knife.

The sauteed vegetables, glistening with butter, were mixed into the bread crumbs with poulty seasoning and sage. The chopped meat was added, and the mixture was dampened with the broth in which the giblets had simmered. Each step was important; shortcuts were not even considered.

The tasting began as the stuffing was mixed. "A little more poultry seasoning," someone advised. "A touch more salt," another said, pinching off another hunk of dressing — it always tasted best when eaten with the fingers.

One year she dared to put chestnuts in the dressing, "Just for something different." Oh, how we complained! We picked out the chestnuts and left them in protest piles on our plates. Another year she slipped in chopped apple. "What did you do to the dressing?" we wailed. "Don't add anything new. Make it the way you always do." In our minds there was no improving perfection.

Mother accomplished her kitchen tasks with great dispatch, no dilly-dallying around, and in quick order she stuffed the bird and sewed up the openings with a big darning needle threaded with string. We considered it a good sign when she slapped the bird's thigh and said, "This is a nice, fat one. It will make good gravy."

While the bird sizzled and roasted, the other preparations were under way. The candied sweet potatoes were readied, the white potatoes peeled, the tomato aspic jelled, and the Brussels sprouts waited to be cooked.

The relish tray was put together last so the carrot and celery sticks, the green onions and red radishes, were at their peak of crispness, the sweet pickles and hot peppers were properly chilled, and the olives — both black and green — were glistening with juice. The tray was then fringed with parsley. Mother was always big on parsley.

By this time the dirty dishes and the pots and pans rose to an alarming height in the sink. Mother usually took care of those while my sister Kay and I set the table, which was moved into the living room for the occasion. We spread the lace cloth and used the good dishes — the Franciscan china with the gold grape design, and the crystal goblets. Three people got place settings of sterling silver. The others had to make do with silverplate. This was a time for "real" napkins, and candles.

Our guests took their places around the table and thanks were given; a hush fell over the room, disturbed only by the sounds of spoons and forks serving up the bounty.

Around the table went the turkey platter, again and again. We loved the white meat, the dark meat, and the crispy skin. We loved the dressing, oh, so right! the mashed potatoes, the gravy, the cranberry sauce — the everything!

Mother's favorite part of the bird was the oyster, the tenderloin from the two small pockets on the turkey's lower back. She saved that for a late night snack after all the guests were gone, when the mouth — but not the stomach — wanted one more bite of turkey.

We each got one mouthful of the succulent oyster, all the more desirable because it was so small. That was followed by a nip of cold dressing and a slice of pumpkin chiffon pie. We were truly happy.

There never was a Thanksgiving without turkey.

NEIGHBORS

Certain names and places from childhood never leave you. Names and places, more recent in time, fade quickly, never to return, but those from long ago cling fast and endure.

Maitland Werig is a name that endures, and it is hard to remember why. He did not often join in our neighborhood games. He was a loner, an only child, and fatherless. His hair was black and his skin very white, maybe because he spent so much time indoors. The house he lived in was long and narrow, part log, part frame, with tall trees in the front yard which sapped the soil so even the quack grass was patchy and sparse. We rarely saw anyone go in or out of the house. The only activity around there was of the clothes swaying and puffing on the clothesline.

Any conversations with Maitland Werig or his tall, black-haired mother, Eleanor, are lost forever, but the names are never erased.

Robbie Weidemeier's name endures too. Robbie lived two doors down from us in a low, sprawling log house. His mother, Virginia, was tall and slender and walked with her head up, proud and regal. Her husband was killed in the war, and her job took her from home for long periods. That left Robbie's upbringing to his grandmother and his aunt, Bea Wolfe. Her hair was platinum, like spun sugar, and she wore it in an elegant French roll. Her hands were soft and white, and she painted her nails with a dark, glossy polish.

Children of assorted age and size, their parents and their homes, made the neighborhood and the childhood memories that endure.

Bea worked ladies-ready-to-wear at the Northern Commercial Company. She wore stylish dark suits, and chic dresses with matching shoes, and full-length coats with full collars and deep cuffs. Every evening she passed our house on her way home from work, recognizable from a distance by her lovely hair and dignified stroll.

Robbie was tall and slender like his mother. He was the same age as my sister Bonnie, whom he adored, but then everyone did. She was a picture-book child with long, golden curls, and big blue eyes. She was small-boned and appealing in her daintiness and her sweet disposition. Daddy called her Platypuss, his term of endearment.

Platypuss is not a name you can easily forget, and neither is Bunny Beebe. She was a roly-poly girl with dark, curly hair and rosy cheeks, the only child of an older couple. Bunny was younger than our gang, but we played with her because she had lots of toys, a dog, candy and spending money — all the things we never had. Her father, a stout, happy-hearted man named Herb, worked for the railroad. Frances, her mother, also stout, spent a lot of time in the bedroom with the drapes drawn.

Their house was log with large rooms; the living room and dining room ran its full length. The furniture was new, and the drapes were lined and pleated. All the rooms except the kitchen had carpets on the floor. The house was built close to the sidewalk, leaving little space for a front yard, but out back where the tall, dark spruces grew was a swing set, a bicycle, a playhouse. We ran in and out of the Beebe house at whim; no one ever told us we should not.

On the same block was Pat Hill's house. It, too, was part log, part frame, with a large, screened front porch that made the living room very dark because it covered the only windows. Pat, who was in my class at school, was an only child and had lost her father when she was about ten, as I had. There was only one bedroom in the house, so Pat slept on a studio couch in the living room. I envied her arrangement, it seemed so grown-up, better than sharing a bedroom with both an older and a younger sister — or so I thought at the time.

The kitchen was in the frame addition, a long, narrow room with tall windows and a sunny corner for the table. There was a wood stove at one end, and next to it a large white wall-hung sink. I loved to help with the dishes at Pat's house because they had Ivory Flakes, and we never did. The soap fell into the water like snowflakes and billowed up into a million bubbles, probably because we used too much. The dishes were kept in a cabinet with glass doors next to the sink. A small room off to the side was the pantry where the canned goods were stored.

Why did someone else's house seem more interesting than one's own?

The bathroom was large enough to accommodate a full-length tub with claw feet, a sink, a toilet bowl, and a wide set of stairs that led to the attic. At the far end of the attic was a diamond-shaped window that overlooked the Chena River.

That's what I mean about scenes from childhood — sometimes the memories are so strong they have to be emptied out, and what better place than in a book where the memory is given new life, where it will endure long after the writer is gone, and the house too.

CHRISTMAS BOXES

About the first week in December, the Christmas box from Grandpa arrived — a little too early, because it made the waiting all the more agonizing. This premature delivery led to some

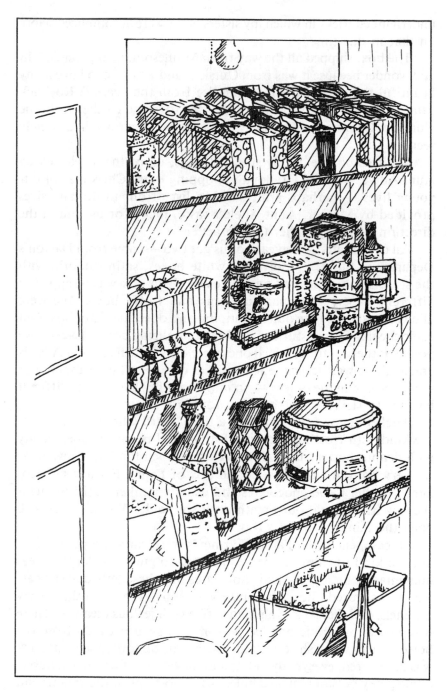

Grandpa's Christmas gifts were stashed in the pantry, but little girls found creative ways to shorten the wait for opening day.

underhanded tricks in which my sisters and I were accomplices. More on that in due time.

The box, shipped all the way from Minnesota, held great delight and wonder because it was from Outside, and was sure to have many beautiful things, not the merchandise from the Sears & Roebuck catalog we had paged for weeks, nor the toys and clothes from the Northern Commercial Company that everybody in town had already seen.

No, this box held only special things, all of them selected by Aunt Adele, who did Grandpa's shopping every Christmas of our young lives — perhaps armed with a list of our up-to-date sizes provided by Mother. Aunt Adele's taste, lucky for us, ran in the direction of pretty rather than practical.

All of our gifts — and each of us got two — came from Dayton's Department Store, in individual white boxes, satin smooth, with the store's name, printed on the cover. Each box was wrapped in different paper, with matching tags and fluffy bows. We were allowed to tear off the outer wrapping and open the outer box. Out came the newspaper stuffing, and the tantalizing boxes. Eagerly we peered at the tags to see which ones were ours. Much to Aunt Adele's credit, there was never the feeling that one got a better looking or bigger box than the others — an important but sometimes difficult balance to strike when shopping for three sisters.

Tucked among the gifts was a tin of hard Christmas candies, the kind with frosting and fruit filling, and peanut shaped candy with peanut butter inside. Mother let us open that right away. At the very bottom was a five-pound box of Fanny Farmer's chocolates. Mother loved chocolates and usually weakened the moment she saw it. We held our breath until she said, "We might as well open the Fannie Farmer's too."

Once opened, the Fannie Farmer's were carefully guarded — not the kind of thing we passed around to guests — let them eat homemade candies. We had chocolates like these only once a year, and we savored the rich, buttery creams, the smooth, chewy caramels, and the slabs of almond toffee with jealous pleasure. There was always one underhanded person who swiped candy from the bottom layer when she didn't like what was on top. Once that trick was discovered, everybody did it, and the box went down in a hurry. Some picky person punched holes in the bottoms of the creams and tossed back the orange and raspberry until they were all that remained.

The arrival of Grandpa's box was our incentive to get his gift in the mail. That was never easy. Both Grandpa and Aunt Adele came under the heading of "Hard to Buy For." Through the years they got their share of gold nugget, ivory and jade jewelry, ivory-handled steak knives, carving sets, and Alaskan oil paintings. Mother could not bring herself to ship gifts to the relatives that they could buy out there, so we kept buying "something Alaskan," knowing full well they did not appreciate the value of baleen boats or grass baskets. They could not have looked forward to our gifts as much as we did to theirs.

Until we put the tree up, the gifts Grandpa sent were stashed in the pantry with the electric roaster, the vacuum cleaner, the canned goods and the ragbag. My sisters and I puzzled over our gift boxes. What was it this year? A pleated skirt, an angora sweater, maybe a purse — hope it's not a nightgown!

We knew we must not open our gifts before December 25, but we did devise a plan that somewhat satisfied our sense of "right-ness" and our curiosity at the same time. Kay and I went into the pantry and opened Bonnie's presents while she waited in the hallway. After we rewrapped her packages — as good as new (almost) — Bonnie and Kay huddled in the pantry to look at my gifts. Next Bonnie and I looked at Kay's gifts. That way all the presents had been opened, but not by the person for whom they were intended.

Then we began the game of "Guess what you got," giving a few creative clues to keep things interesting. That could go on for several days until all the secrets were out. Since we had not actu-ally seen our own gifts, we could muster up enough enthusiasm to act surprised on Christmas morning. I doubt that Mother was fooled.

HOTEL de GINK

C ould it be that the downtown apartment house my uncle owned did not have a name? As I recall there was no sign over the door, but it didn't need one; everybody knew where it was. The two-story building faced Cushman Street where Woolworth's stands today. There were small shops — a beauty parlor, bookstore and ladies' ready-to-wear — on the ground floor, and eight or ten apart-ments upstairs. My Uncle Sig, in his good-humored way, called the place Hotel de Gink.

Handsome, good-humored Uncle Sig could hold his liquor, tell a good story and sing, and he never missed a day's work.

We entered through a large glass door and immediately mounted a very wide and long flight of stairs that went straight to the top without pause for a landing. I believe ten people abreast could have climbed those stairs without being crowded. But wait, maybe my perception is faulty and the stairs only appeared so wide to a five-year-old girl.

Dark linoleum, held firmly in place by metal strips, covered the stairs. Every footfall, even the tap-tap of my little patent leather shoes, echoed noisily on the stairs and down the empty hallway.

The hallway was long and dark. The only light was from bare bulbs hung on cords from the ceiling. They burned day and night but produced more shadows than light. It was always nighttime at Hotel de Gink.

I could have gone into the apartment house blindfolded and known immediately where I was. Every building has its own mingling of odors. As soon as I reached the top stair it hit me, that blend of old wood and furniture polish, of cigarette smoke and bottled gas, the frying of steaks and onions.

My aunt contributed to the tantalizing blend because she cooked with exotic spices — paprika and thyme; she shot streams of Worcestershire into the soup, and wine into the beef stew. Her lemon pie had pure almond extract in the meringue; her spareribs and sauerkraut simmered to a delectable tenderness flavored with bits of brown sugar. She put Tabasco sauce on her scrambled eggs!

When she cooked it was like a conductor directing a symphony orchestra. She brought the various parts together with precision, and the rhythmic movement of her round arms and graceful hands. At the same time her long earrings would swing to a different tune.

In the clutter of Auntie's kitchen cupboard were gin, Vermouth and white pearl onions for her martinis, and Uncle Sig's bottle of Scotch. I suppose the odor of alcohol was also part of the Hotel de Gink's bouquet.

Their apartment was small, only two rooms, with high ceilings and a skylight in the kitchen to make up for the absence of windows. We entered through the kitchen, which was crowded with a sink, cupboards, refrigerator and gas stove. The gas stove had black burners and brass fittings on the knobs and a flame that shot up blue and orange. It also gave off a peculiar odor.

The white enamel sink was stained from the rusty water that came out of the spigots. It was not fit to drink, so water was delivered once a week, in a large glass bottle, from Pioneer Wells.

Auntie had a set of sterling silver which she used every day, and a beautiful service of dishes — Wild Rose by Franciscan. All the dishes matched, even the bowls, the small plates, the gravy boat, the sugar bowl and creamer.

The other room, which had windows across the front and over-looked the main street, was the bedroom and sitting room. It was very small and crowded, trying to be too many things all at once. Behind glass doors on one side of the room was a double bed folded against the wall. Before the bed could be lowered, all the furniture had to be rearranged — tables, lamps, and chairs — night after night, like shifting scenery for a play. When the bed was down there was precious little room for walking around.

At Hotel de Gink none of the apartments had bathroom facili-ties. You went down the hall and to the left. When Auntie made that trip she said she had to "squizzle," a wonderfully descriptive word, almost as good as her "Judas Priest," which she pronounced with great expression.

Very often when we came calling, Auntie was seated at the card table in the living room, her make-up and hair exquisitely done, playing solitaire. She had pale pink skin, and small hands with beau-tifully shaped nails religiously manicured. She dressed stylishy but always lamented her plump figure, a contrast to my uncle's wiry frame.

My uncle never seemed to change; he always looked trim and fit, and a shade shorter than my aunt when she wore high heels. He had a fine head of hair — silver gray, full and wavy and neatly cut. He was smooth-shaven and had a network of broken blood vessels across his cheeks and nose. Years ago, while running his dog team taxi from McCarthy to the Kennecott mines, he had been severely frost-bitten.

My uncle was a handsome man; the ladies liked him, and yet he was a man's man. He could hold his liquor and tell a good story, and he never missed a day's work. He was the life of the party and, with a little coaxing, he would burst into song. "Little Brown Jug" was our favorite. "Sing it again," we pleaded until he finally broke away, a big smile on his face as he ran for the door.

With no trouble at all I can conjure up the days at the old Hotel de Gink, where my shoes went tappity-tap on the linoleum, where the hallway was mysteriously dark and aromatic, where the steam pipes thumped in the night, and where my sisters and I tried out daring new words like "squizzle" and "Judas Priest."

SUMMER AT THE SPRINGS

A vacation in those days meant a trip to some place within driving distance, and since the highway to Anchorage had not yet been built, the choice was reduced to three: Harding Lake, Birch Lake or The Springs. To us there was only one springs and that was Circle Hot Springs, a spa one hundred fifty miles north almost to the Arctic Circle.

Frank Leach homesteaded the property in 1905 and it became the most popular resort in the North, both summer and winter. Before long an imposing three-and-a-half-story white clapboard hotel was built in the middle of the wilderness. The miners from the Circle District liked to soak their tired limbs in the hundred thirty-nine degree water that bubbled out of the ground. In addition to the hotel, there were small cabins heated with gravity-flow hot water, where the miners could stay warm without chopping a single stick of firewood.

During the summer the Springs were the playground for people from Fairbanks who came up to swim and relax. In 1948, after my father's death, Mother took a summer job waiting on tables at the hotel. I think she did that so my sisters and I could have a vacation and she could make enough money to keep us together. Kay and I were eleven and ten, respectively, and Bonnie was five. We had three glorious months of cabin living, of swimming, hiking, horseback riding and eating at the hotel dining room.

Many of my memories of that summer concern food. The dining room was — and is — long and narrow, with a low ceiling and small windows set rather high. There was a wide aisle with a runner carpet, and long wooden tables each seating eight, on both sides of the aisle. Food was served family style and believe me, people began lining up early to get a seat. As I recall there were two sittings for each meal.

The food was your basic meat and potatoes, with the emphasis on fresh vegetables grown in the huge garden adjacent to the hotel, where the soil was warmed by underground pipes circulating water from the hot springs. Of course the vegetables thrived under such conditions and early in the season the garden produced leaf lettuce, green onions and radishes. They were followed by an array of cauliflower, beet greens, head lettuce, turnips, rutabagas, carrots, cabbages, green beans, peas and kohlrabi.

There were two large greenhouses stuffed full of tomatoes and

"The Springs" still means Circle Hot Springs Resort, pioneered in 1905 and still popular in both summer and winter.

cucumbers, and in the surrounding fields were acres of potatoes. Every bowl of whipped potatoes served in the dining room had its start in that patch. Overseeing this abundance of vegetables was the full-time gardener who also found time to plant flowers along the garden fence.

Since Mother worked there, we took all of our meals in the dining room, but for guests in the cottages there was a grocery store. The summer we were there Ruth and John Berdahl, a handsome young couple with three children, ran the hotel and store. I thought the Berdahl children were wonderfully blessed to have parents who owned a grocery store, where cookies and candy were theirs for the taking.

Charlotte Anne, who worked as a chambermaid for four years during the 1930s, said that in those days Fairbanks people flocked to the Springs on the weekends. The Saturday night dance was the star attraction. Or maybe it was the midnight supper featuring ham and turkey, vegetable platters and potato salad, homemade bread and pie — all you could eat for fifty cents. Charlotte did some moonlighting as piano player at the dances and that, along with her maid's work, earned her seventy-five dollars a month, plus room and board.

Mr. and Mrs. Leach operated the hotel in those days. Mrs. Leach washed and ironed (on a mangle) all the sheets and table linen used by the guests, which often reached the resort's capacity of one hundred fifty.

One year there was an ice-cream parlor in a cabin near the hotel, where guests sat on the screened porch eating ice cream freighted in from Fairbanks. Cold storage was achieved by putting the ice cream and frozen meats in an ice cave behind the hotel.

There was an outdoor swimming pool down the road a short way from the hotel. It had cribbed sides, a mud floor and a diving board, and was used when the weather was nice and the mosquitoes bearable. The smell of sulphur was pervasive there. My sisters and I thought it smelled like rotten eggs and we did a lot of gagging and holding of our noses until we got used to the odor. Next to the hotel were the bathhouse and indoor pool and the soaking pools of temperatures one hundred twenty degrees and more. The swimming pool had a very rough cement finish that hurt our hands and elbows when we bumped against it.

A young girl drowned in the outdoor swimming pool one summer. The funeral was held in the hotel lobby. The resident carpenter built the coffin, which the chambermaids decked with wildflowers. The young male employees, dressed in their Sunday suits, carried the coffin on their shoulders up the hill to the cemetery, where Mr. and Mrs. Leach have since been laid to rest. Even now beautiful blue and purple lupine spread their colors across the faded markers.

FAMILY FRIENDS

Our world of growing up in Fairbanks was inhabited with kids our age, of course, and plenty of them, but also with older people, those wonderful friends of the family who added another dimension to our lives, and live now in memory only.

My sisters and I were fortunate that our parents had the good judgment to select as friends couples without children. Childless couples tend to elevate children to a special realm. We were the recipients of costly fruits and candies, of extravagant toys and fanciful clothes. We were doted on, fussed over, babied and spoiled, and we loved every minute of it.

Across the street from our log cabin at Third and State was a two-story frame house where Frances and Smitty Smith lived. They had heavy drapes at the windows, rugs on the floor, a central heating system, an affluent spread of furniture and gadgets. The Smiths were in a class of their own in our neighborhood.

Smitty was tall, a dapper gentleman most often dressed in a gray suit, gray vest and white shirt. He wore a heavy gold ring on his little finger — a mark of distinction in our book. His hair was white, brushed back, and he had a long, straight, aristocratic nose. When he wasn't smoking a cigar he was chewing one, but he came by that quite naturally as the owner of the Horseshoe Cigar Store.

My sister Kay and I went to the cigar store from time to time on the pretext of a visit, but really for a handout of the candy and gum displayed in the glass case. Possibly we had the good sense not to overdo it. We were always made to feel welcome, though the Smiths were no doubt aware of our motives.

In the card room, behind the swinging doors, we glimpsed the serious-faced men grouped around the table, heads bent over their hands, and we heard the slap-slap of the cards on the green felt cover. A serious silence prevailed. Watching the action, under a cloud of cigar smoke, was Smitty.

Frances worked in the cigar store too, and was equally generous in treating us. Where Smitty was tall, Frances was short; where he was gray, she was blonde; where he was slim, she was not, but they were a happy couple. He treated her like a queen, lavishing on her beautiful jewelry, mostly rings, and a watch with diamonds even we knew was of great value.

Having no children of their own, Frances and Smitty had an unused store of patience and forgiveness toward my sisters and me. They didn't even get irritated when we painted their woodpile green and pulled up the rhubarb in their backyard.

Another favorite downtown spot was the Star Liquor Store, next to the Pioneer Hotel on First Avenue, which happened to be on our way home from town. Tommy and Rilla Morgan owned it. He was a heavy-equipment operator who frequently worked out of town, so our contact was more often with Rilla. We were a little in awe of her because she was impeccably well groomed. Her smooth, dark hair was combed in a page boy, and she wore tailored suits and pure white blouses of some satiny material. She had a deep, throaty voice, and as soon as she spoke we knew we were in the presence of someone who liked us.

Very often Rilla was seated behind the counter, waiting for customers. If she waved us in that could mean a free Coke, or a chance on the punchboard, or — happy day — both. The board had holes drilled in it which we punched with a metal key, and out came a curled-up piece of paper. If the paper had the right combination of lemons, cherries and bells, we would be in the big money. Somehow that never happened, but we were happy enough living in hopes.

When our parents took us to Rilla and Tommy's apartment for dinner, we were treated to steak and French fries, and Coca Cola served in tall glasses with tinkling ice cubes. Tommy, a jovial, big-hearted man, gave us piggyback rides until he nearly collapsed from exhaustion.

We also had several surrogate uncles — old-timers who had escaped family ties by coming to the North — who "adopted" us as the children they never had. These friends of the family acted in lieu of our relatives in faraway Duluth and Superior, whom we rarely saw. We were on our best behavior for our "stand-in" uncles, so how could they know little girls were not always sugar and spice?

Fred Panachek was more of an uncle to the Cohoe kids than he was to us, but when we saw his car parked in front of their house we knew we would share in his generosity that knew no limits. He bought boxes of chocolates and the first watermelon of the season. He could be counted on for ice cream several times a week, and he was very likely to hand out money on a come-and-get-it basis.

Fred was a slender fellow of Slavic descent, with a bony face and dark, thinning hair. He worked at some lonely job at Point Barrow, and when he came to town with a pocketful of money he was ready for a party. He treated his adult friends with the same reckless extravagance he showered on us.

Tiny Conrad also filled a niche in our lives. He was uncle, big brother and year-round Santa Claus all in one. He was a big man, broad-shouldered and hefty. His laugh was jolly, his eyes merry, and his pockets were filled with silver dollars which he handed to us as if they were poker chips. One time he gave me a roll which I very carefully unwrapped and counted — twenty silver dollars!

Each time Tiny left our house, my sisters and I made a beeline for the big chair where he had been sitting. We pulled out the cushions and felt down deep in the cracks for the stray coins that had slipped out of his pockets. Somehow the money we found meant more than what Tiny had given us. We blew every penny on licorice bits and root-beer balls.

Let us not forget Sig, our only real uncle who lived in Fairbanks. He bounced us on his knee, and accused my sisters and me — much to our horror — of biting off his missing finger. To this day we don't know how he lost it.

He was a fun-loving gregarious man with a quick wit and happy smile. Uncle Sig had a wonderful singing voice, too, and we loved to sing with him. He knew hundreds of songs — turn-of-the-century ditties like "When You Wore A Tulip," "Bicycle Built For Two," "I Want A Girl," and "Daisy, Daisy." Whenever I hear them I think of Uncle Sig.

Is growing up in other places full of uncles and old-timers and family friends and their wonderful gifts of love?

Destinies

Adolph and Cleora Casady were nine and five when they joined their father at Goldstream in 1906. Cleora never left Alaska.

Destinies

CLEORA REMEMBERS

This story of Cleora Casady Bachner Erickson is taken from her unpublished autobiography.

I was five years old in 1906, when I stepped off the boat in Fairbanks with my mother and nine-year-old brother, Adolph. We came to join my father, who was mining on Goldstream. A friend of his met us at the landing and carried me on his shoulders all the way to that creek town.

When winter set in we moved to Fairbanks. For the next few years we lived in a log cabin chinked with moss, with a pole roof topped with sod — an ideal playground for the spiders that frequently landed on my brother and me. Mother collected paper to tack on the walls by our bunks, to protect us.

The beds were two long pole shelves, one on top of the other, extending from wall to wall at the far end of the cabin. A foot of dried grass was spread over the poles, and topped with a feather bed. Early in the evening Mother heated the flatirons on the stove, and then wrapped them in many thicknesses of paper and placed them at the foot of our beds. They added greatly to our comfort on cold winter nights when the bedclothes often froze to the outside walls.

The Yukon stove was the center of life in the cabin. At times Adolph and I felt it was a monster, designed to consume endless armfuls of pole wood we had to dig out of the snowbank and pack into the house. And yet we knew that the stove was necessary to cook the meals, melt the ice and snow for water, and keep the house warm.

We had little in the way of furniture. A homemade table sat beneath one small window, and four stacked egg cases in the corner served as a cupboard. Mother sewed flour sacks for curtains. There were wooden milk cases for chairs, and an armless rocker. I have no idea how we came to have the "elegant" piece, but Mother took a great deal of pride in it and made a fancy little cushion for the seat.

The outhouse was a gunny-sack-covered pole affair in the willow patch behind the cabin. The thoughtful builder had upholstered the seat with caribou hide, fur side up. Believe me, that was appreciated on cold winter days.

In the backyard were eight dog houses, each with a malemute chained in front. Some of these dogs were vicious and Adolph and I were told to stay well away from them. Caribou, moose, bear or other wild meat Father brought home was used to feed the dogs. This meat, and sometimes smoked salmon, was cooked with yellow oatmeal on the back of the Yukon stove.

Father was a big six-footer with red hair and blue eyes. He had a grand voice for singing Irish tunes and was very charming when so inclined. But Father had another side which he reserved mostly for family life. We never knew when he would go off on a week's drinking spree. There never was a shortage of drinks for him; he sang for his whiskey. The saloon-keepers were happy to see him come and glad to furnish him drinks as long as he was willing and able to sing. His rollicking Irish songs drew a crowd and business boomed.

When he became too liquor-laden to sing and his disposition soured, the saloon-keeper sent him home to us, usually late in the night. When Mother heard him coming she hid Adolph and me under the bed. Poor little Mother, many a black-and-blue mark she tried to cover up and pretend it never happened.

A few days after Thanksgiving that first winter in Fairbanks, Father hooked up his dog team to a large basket sled, loaded it with his winter camping outfit, and took off. That was after he had cleaned out the food in the cabin and the money Mother had managed to save. Just before he cracked the whip over the backs of the malemutes, he said to Mother, "Get busy and rustle a job so you can feed the kids."

The nicest things I can remember about Father were his absences. Mother took in sewing, nursed the sick, or waited on table to earn a few dollars. She was a neat little person with a kind, cheerful face and blue eyes. Her dark brown hair hung below her knees in a braid as thick as a man's wrist.

Adolph and I were delighted to be left alone with Mother. We kept the wood box stacked and the fifty-pound butter keg behind the stove filled with ice, which melted during the night, providing water for the next day. Chunks of ice, cut from the Chena River, were stacked like cordwood in our backyard. They produced more water than melting snow.

When the evening chores were finished, the three of us played games and sang songs, and Mother told us of her early life in Canada. She sat in the little rocking chair, her knitting needles clicking as she talked, and the Yukon stove warmed us all.

Garden Island School

In the spring of 1907, as soon as the ground around the cabin was free of snow, Mother, Adolph and I spaded the soil and mixed in manure for a vegetable garden. A bonus crop was the lovely little mushrooms that popped up every time it rained. Mother gathered them the minute they showed above the ground. Those mushrooms made us happy to see the showers come.

In the backyard a high bank dropped steeply into the slough, a branch of the Chena River. Occasionally rowboats and poling boats strayed up the slough and caused excitement for the children who lived along the bank. And even though Mother forbade it, Adolph and I went swimming in the brackish water.

A big event in the summer was the arrival of the cattle barge on the Chena. The steers, sheep and pigs were unloaded at the dock near the Cushman Street bridge and herded to the stock pens at Birch Hill. After the long journey the stock was wild and hard to manage. The cattle-drivers were soon shouting and going at a wild gallop, and sending their dogs out to hold the herd together. The barking of the dogs, the flying hooves, the squealing of the pigs and the bleating of the sheep, all this was great entertainment.

The animals were herded out to Birch Hill and kept in pole corrals until time for the slaughterhouse. Adolph and I went out there as often as we could, to hang on the fence and feed wild grass to the steers.

On that same hill grew wonderful blueberries. Mother took us there to help her pick the berries, which she sold to restaurants. We often took a picnic lunch and spent the day.

Mother had no difficulty disposing of her berries; she picked them so clean they sold on sight. It wasn't unusual for her to pick thirty pounds each day. When the restaurant orders were filled, Adolph and I sold the remaining berries door to door for twenty-five cents a pound.

We picked berries for our own use too. It was Adolph's and

The little red schoolhouse on Garden Island had one room, a couple of dozen pupils, and a series of harried teachers.

my job to gather empty glass bottles and make them into jelly jars. This we did by cutting lengths of string soaked in coal oil, and wrapping the string around the top of the bottle. The string was set on fire, and as soon as it burned the bottle was dunked into a pail of cold water, causing the glass to crack where the heat had weakened it. A slight tap, and the top fell away. We smoothed the rough edges with a rasp, and the container was ready for use. Melted paraffin was used to seal the jar.

That winter was a long, hard one. Once again Father took all the food and money and took off for parts unknown. Mother saw to it that we had enough to eat, never fancy, but filling. She made my dresses from hand-me-downs, and for years my underwaists and petticoats were made from flour sacks.

One day several members of the Pioneer Lodge called at our little cabin to offer Mother aid to see us through the winter. They were being kind, of course, but Mother was insulted. She told them we would make it on our own, and we did.

I was six that year, eager for that wonderful day when I could start school. Our Garden Island schoolhouse was a one-room frame building on the slough a quarter of a mile upstream from our cabin. The outside was painted a brick red. Inside were two rows of desks with an aisle up the middle. The grades were from one to eight, but not all grades had pupils. There were about two dozen children attending school.

The big boys took turns arriving early in the morning to light the fire in the tank stove. They also filled pails with ice chunks and placed them beside the stove to melt. That provided water for drinking and washing. On a stand nearby was a tin wash basin and a drinking cup. When the weather was bitterly cold the pupils farthest from the heat would get chilly, so class would be delayed while everyone cuddled up to the stove.

During my two years at the little red schoolhouse I remember several teachers and the struggles they had trying to keep order. Some of the older boys were bigger than the teacher and enjoyed teasing her. One teacher kept a small buggy whip locked in her desk as a persuader. She had to get a replacement several times after the old one disappeared. No one had the slightest idea what had become of it. Of course, we all knew who had picked the lock, swiped the whip, cut it in little pieces and buried it in the snow, but not even the smallest first-grader (me) would tell. It was thoroughly understood that everyone hated a tattletale.

Christmas On the Creek

In 1908 my parents were divorced. Adolph, who was my father's son by a former marriage, went to Valdez with him. I missed my brother desperately. Mother got a job waiting on tables at a gold mine on Engineer Creek. We lived in a small room in the back of a house occupied by the mine owner and his wife, Mr. and Mrs. Henning. Our room was frugally furnished with a double bed, a bureau and wash basin, a small table and one chair, and a stack of egg crates to serve as shelves.

It was a long and lonely winter for an eight-year-old girl. Mother worked long hours and I was alone all day. The mine owner's wife was not the sort to bother much with children. I never entered their quarters except by invitation, which was seldom extended. We borrowed books from the school in Fairbanks and I was supposed to do my daily lessons, but I'm afraid my education that winter was almost a total loss. Much of my time I spent looking at old magazines and cutting out paper dolls.

I also spent many hours standing on a milk box peering out one corner of the frosty pane. Several times a day teams of horses went by, hauling huge loads of birch and spruce wood to the boilerhouse. Occasionally a dog team would pass, or a horse-drawn cutter. Mother served meals to one hundred fifty workers in the mess hall. I watched them come and waited anxiously for them to leave, because that was my signal to go to the mess hall and eat with Mother — the best part of the day.

I was fascinated by the conversation of the Japanese cooks and kitchen helpers. It seemed to me they all talked at the same time and nobody listened. Even when they spoke English I could hardly understand a thing they said. They were very kind to me, and it would have been such fun to stay and visit, but Mother said, "No, you talk too much and ask too many questions. Run along and I will be home soon."

Christmas was drawing near, but it didn't mean much to me. Adolph was gone, and I wouldn't be at school or church to take part in the programs. I loved those celebrations and the beautiful Christmas tree, and the excitement of giving my recitation in the front of the room, wearing my starched white dress and long white stockings. I was consoled by the fact that the Henning Mine would close for three days to give the miners time to celebrate Christmas in Fairbanks, and Mother would not have to work.

As Christmas neared I became aware of unusual activity in the owner's part of the house. Mother said the Hennings were having a Christmas Eve party, and we were invited. I could hardly wait. The hour finally came. Mother knocked on the door and Mrs. Henning called, "Come in."

We walked through the door into an enchanted fairyland. The room was brightly lighted and decorated. In one corner stood a spruce tree covered with store-bought trimmings — not a single paper chain or popcorn string.

I — the chatterbox — was speechless, and could only stand and stare. I couldn't believe what I saw under the tree — a beautiful doll, with real eyelashes and long curls, wearing a lace-trimmed pink dress and white shoes. I had never owned a doll. All my life I had yearned for one, but even in my dreams I had not pictured one so beautiful as the doll Mrs. Henning placed in my arms. That is a moment I will remember forever. I loved that doll dearly and named her Annabelle.

The next day there was a steady stream of callers to our little room. From midafternoon until late at night they came, and Mother would open the door to find a bashful miner standing outside in the snow. Each handed her a package and said, "Just wanted to bring the little girl a present."

I was busy all day unwrapping packages. When the last caller departed, Mother and I surveyed the gifts. There were sixty boxes of chocolates, and one hand-embroidered silk handkerchief from Japan.

The remainder of the winter went much faster with Annabelle for company.

In the early summer the Henning Mine was closed. We moved to 17 Below Goldstream, where Mother was a housekeeper for the mine owner and his wife.

Ester Creek and Uncle Jim

We moved often, following the gold strikes where Mother could get work and room and board for us both. In 1910 we were living on St. Patrick's Creek, four miles from the thriving town of Ester. There were two white Siberian huskies in camp, and it didn't take me long to make friends with them. I was allowed to hitch the dogs to the sled, as Adolph had taught me to do, and take them for a ride around camp. As I got braver I ventured farther and farther down the trail. When the mine-owner needed someone to go to Ester once a week to get the mail and a few items at the store, I convinced him I could do it. On those days I left the camp at daybreak and wasted no time along the way. Darkness fell early, and I wanted to be back home before the precious light was gone. When I didn't make it, I would crawl onto the sled, tell the dogs to go home, pull the fur robe over my head, and hope for the best.

The dogs were as anxious as I was to get home, and they trotted at a fast clip until a rabbit jumped in front of them and they gave chase. I often got dumped and had to drag the sled back onto the trail, find my parcels in the snow, and get the team started again.

That winter I was ten and I missed another year of school, but my great love for reading continued to grow. Many of the words in the books and magazines were beyond my understanding, but I plowed through them anyway. While my schoolwork suffered, I was gaining knowledge about gold-mining. I took trips down the mine shaft, and through the tunnels where the miners were digging gravel by the light of a flickering candle. I pestered the men with questions, and hoped someday I might strike it rich.

When we moved to Ester Siding the following summer, Mother did the cooking and cleaning at the roadhouse. She taught me to help with the sweeping, dusting, dishwashing and small cooking jobs. She got up at five in the morning to mix bread dough and prepare the pies and cakes. There were seven steady boarders as well as drop-in trade. A narrow-gauge railroad operated between Fairbanks and Chatanika, carrying freight and passengers to the mining camps en route. The supplies and travelers destined for Ester got off at the siding and took the stage twelve miles to Ester.

The Ester Creek stage driver became a good friend of ours. Jim was a tall, handsome Irishman with black curly hair, a charming personality, and a heart of gold. For many years I called this man Uncle Jim, and the memories of him run like a golden thread across the dull gray cloth of my childhood years.

Early in our acquaintance I decided he was the man I wanted for my stepfather. I told Mother, "Uncle Jim is the nicest person we know. Wouldn't he be a wonderful stepfather?"

Mother patted my head and smiled as she answered: "There are many things you won't understand until you are much older, and this is one of them. I'm sure your Uncle Jim will always be one of our best friends."

I tried working on Uncle Jim in a roundabout way. He agreed with me that Mother was a "nice lady," and "a pretty little woman" and "a very good cook," but all my efforts were in vain. Here were the two most wonderful people in my world, and they weren't in the least bit interested in each other. Funny people, these grownups.

The following summer we moved to Ester. Mother was a waitress at the cafe. There was a little red schoolhouse, closed for lack of children although several hundred people lived on the creek at that time. Mother did not want me to miss another year of school, so in the fall Uncle Jim took me to Ester Siding to catch the train for Fairbanks. I stayed with a family in town during the week and returned home on Friday afternoons.

The highlights of that winter were my rides on the stage twice a week with Uncle Jim. He let me sit on the front seat next to him, taking special care that I was well wrapped in the fur robe. Uncle Jim would tell me about his boyhood in Ireland, and the early days in Dawson, where he was a stage-driver. When he ran out of stories he would sing. How I loved to hear him sing!

When spring came we watched for the small grouse chicks or little rabbits along the road. I have seen Uncle Jim bring the stage to a halt while a grouse led her flock to safety, or climb down and gently shoo baby rabbits out of the way before driving on. Sometimes the passengers became impatient at the delay, or made fun of Uncle Jim. He always responded cheerfully, "If the stage is too slow, you can always walk."

That summer someone gave Uncle Jim a bear cub he had found in the woods. Uncle Jim kept him chained to the side of the stable. The cub grew vary tame and friendly. He loved to eat blueberries with sugar and drink the beer the men gave him. He had a small blanket he used to cover himself. It was funny to see the cub stand on his hind feet and shake his blanket before stretching out on the ground and pulling the blanket down with his hind feet and up with his front paws. With closed eyes he pretended to sleep, but at the slightest sound he would leap up on all fours and be ready to play again.

The bear loved to wrestle and some of the younger fellows enjoyed giving him a workout, until he became too strong for them. When winter came he dug a deep, dark cave under the stable and, taking his blanket with him, retired for the winter. The following year he broke loose and returned to life in the woods.

Livengood Stampede

Gold was discovered on Livengood Creek, eighty miles northwest of Fairbanks, in the late fall of 1914. By spring the miners had hit paydirt and the boom was on.

Some two thousand men made a dash for the new camp as soon as the waterways opened in May. They went down the Chena and the Tanana to the Tolovana, then upriver to a place called Logjam. There they crossed a narrow strip of land and took the river again to West Fork. After wading several miles through the mud they came to Livengood, originally called Brooks, a cluster of crude shelters on the brow of a hill.

Mother and I were living in Fairbanks and she was married to Jack Nielsen, a handsome sailor from Denmark. He was a good husband and a kind stepfather.

Jack got the gold fever and joined the rush to Livengood. Ten days later he wrote Mother, telling her to get a winter's supply of food and come out on the next boat. We left on September 7, 1915, on the *Shushana*. She was a small riverboat with an engine room, seven tiny staterooms and a galley. Every inch of space was packed with freight and she towed a barge, also loaded, as big as she was. There were three women and fourteen men aboard. I took my dog, Bowser, and a small white kitten.

At seven in the morning the Japanese cook rang the gong and served a fine meal. We stopped to buy fish at a Native fish wheel along the way, and took on six cords of wood at a wood camp. The *Shushana* burned a third of a cord of wood and ran ten downstream miles in an hour.

The Tolovana is a narrow river, running in some stretches through flats with grass to the water's edge and in others, between sheer cliffs with not a sign of life nor a blade of grass. We passed three loaded poling boats going toward Logjam, everyone hoping to get a paying claim. I hoped there would be enough good ground to go around — but there never is.

We were going smoothly upriver when suddenly, BUMP! We had struck a snag and put a hole in the hull. This caused much frantic activity. The water pumps were started, but the water was coming in so fast they didn't do much good. Mother dashed into our stateroom and packed our suitcases, and the men told us to get onto the barge. They untied the barge from the boat, and tied both to large trees on the riverbank.

Much as the crew tried to keep the boat afloat, she sank and sat on the bottom. The river wasn't very deep. The water came up to the main deck, and several cords of wood came floating out of the engine room and sailed down the river.

As soon as everyone was safe, even my white kitten, the men put a gangplank to the deck of the boat, brought food, dishes and chairs ashore, and set up two tents on the bank among the tall cottonwoods, and we all pitched in to make camp.

"We should all be thankful that no lives were lost," said the captain, "not even the cat's. But never so long as I live will I take another cat aboard. They're bad luck, every time."

One of the crew members spoke up, "We had thirteen chairs aboard, and earlier today an owl flew into the boat railing."

So the cat, the owl and the thirteen chairs got blamed for our shipwreck, though I couldn't see that it was the fault of any of them.

That first night we women slept in the barge while the men slept in a tent. The only place we could find to spread our blankets was on a huge pile of sacked oats. They were all hills and hollows in the wrong places, and hard as rocks besides, and not much space between the oats and the roof. We kept bumping our heads when we tried to shift positions.

It kept raining, no sign that it would ever stop, but everyone made the best of things. I enjoyed every minute — but, as Mother said, I wasn't old enough to have any better sense.

Both the salt and the sugar were in one-pound cans, and one day at dinner someone started passing the wrong can. It went the full length of the table, and we all put salt in our tea.

Early in our second afternoon the riverboat *Dan* came by, towing a big barge. The captain said he would deliver his barge to Logjam, then come back for us. Next morning he did. The *Dan* was a small boat, no place for us to stay except the galley or the engine room, and the cook was so cranky, we didn't dare hang out in the galley. There were ninety bales of hay in the engine room, and all we could do was sit and watch the engine work.

On September 14 we got to Logjam, so called because there was a mile-long jam of logs where the river makes a hairpin turn. Boats couldn't pass, so they unloaded their freight on the bit of land inside the turn. The river had risen twenty feet with all that rain, so now the bit of land was in island. The first boats to arrive, their skippers eager to make another trip before freeze-up, had unloaded their freight at the river's edge. Thirty tons of the lighter stuff had already floated away, and the rest was buried under feet of river silt. Still there were more than a hundred and fifty tons of freight on the island, some of it covered with tarpaulins but most of it just sitting there soaking.

We heard that one couple had lost an entire outfit, plus two trunks with all their personal belongings.

There was a tramway almost a mile long to carry the freight past the logjam, where it was loaded onto a small boat and moved another twenty-five miles upriver. I walked over to see the logjam. It was a huge pile of drift logs, in some places fifteen feet high, stretching as far upriver as I could see.

Dad came to meet us and take our freight up to Mike Hess Creek, where he had built a cabin. With him was a man named George Bachner, who'd been in the Livengood country for a year. He as about twenty-two, a fine-looking man all dressed up in a brand new blue overall suit. He was to be our neighbor, only two miles from Dad's cabin.

Dad and some others set up a stove in front of one of the three tents, and Mother cooked for the twelve men in camp. Each brought food from his own store to pay for his supper, and they ate in shifts.

The *Shushana* had sixty-three tons of freight to unload. The captain asked me to keep tally, so I spent the afternoon checking freight. George sat opposite me, also checking freight. Every time I glanced toward him he was watching me. Huh! I thought, I'm too young to be interested in men (I wasn't quite fourteen), and I'm going to be very fussy when I pick a husband. No swearing, no drunkenness and no black-and-blue marks in my married life! Of course, if the man of my choice happened to be a fine young fellow with black, curly hair, like George, I wouldn't mind at all.

The barge and the boat crew went down the Tolovana next morning. We stood on the bank and waved until they were out of sight. I dreaded being left on that muddy riverbank in the middle of nowhere, but the river had fallen two and a half feet, which was some consolation, and we had a big job to do. We had to get our freight to the other side of that land turned island. Part of the tramway was gone with the floodwaters, but a horse-drawn go-devil was hauling freight. By the next morning all our goods were aboard the *Robert E. Lee,* a thirty-foot riverboat with a barge in tow. Boat and barge together carried six tons of freight. Every inch was packed. We sat on a pile of freight.

It was tricky navigating the narrow river overhung with sweepers. There were snags too, and any one of them could knock a hole in the hull. When it got dark we tied up to the shore, the men set up tents, and everyone cut spruce boughs to cover the ground inside the tent. When the boughs were a foot deep, a canvas was spread over them. Each person spread out his bedroll, kicked off his boots, and crawled in for the night.

Our next stop was the Trapper's Cabin, where a lonesome trapper holed up for the winter. Now it was the place where stampeders' freight was transferred to smaller boats. What a sight! Freight piled up along the bank for half a mile! It had been covered with water for several days, and sacks of beans and rice had swollen, burst and begun to sprout. Sodden sacks of flour and sugar lay knee-deep in mud. Boxes of dried fruit had swollen and burst. Piles of oats and hay were green with mold. The air was suffocating with a heavy, sour smell, and with something worse which I could not place until I walked up the bank and saw two dead horses. They had died from eating moldy hay and oats.

It was a relief to leave the sights and smells of such destruction. I still feel like weeping when I think of what those floodwaters did to the prospectors — the losses, the heartaches, the months of toil.

Later in the afternoon we ran into a sweeper that tore a couple of planks off the boat. For a moment it looked as if we were going to sink, but we managed to pull into shore and make repairs.

The next day, September 21, I became fourteen years old, but there was no birthday cake. We were cooking over a campfire and sleeping in a tent at West Fork. From here we would walk fifteen miles to Dad's cabin and our goods would go by pack horse — at twenty-five cents a pound.

West Fork was a new (and short-lived) town consisting of three stores, four warehouses, a roadhouse and forty finished houses strung for half a mile along the riverbank. I counted sixty tents and a dozen half-finished cabins. From all sides came the sounds of saws and hammers, as the big spruce trees were cut for cabin logs. They were beautiful trees, growing about ten feet apart and seventy feet tall.

We rested for four days at West Fork. I went hunting — shot six rabbits and some birds.

Early in the morning of September 25 we began walking. The trail was very winding and very wet. In places we sank to our knees.

Our boots were soon full of water and our feet got icy cold, but all we could do was keep going. Before noon we reached Brooks, the main mining camp on Livengood Creek. There were stores, saloons, dance halls and log cabins, but mostly there were tents, hundreds of them in all directions. There were three thousand people living there, and three-fourths of them must have been living in tents. We stayed overnight to rest and dry our clothes.

Next day, after six more hours of wading mud and swamps and climbing hills, we reached our new home. It was a small, one-room log cabin with a pole roof, moss-covered, a slab door, and one precious window. The furnishings were wooden packing boxes for chairs and cupboards, a table with pole legs and a whipsawed board on top, and two pole beds, a large one at one end for Mother and Dad and a narrow one at the other end for me. The yard was willows, moss and rabbit trails, with Mike Hess Creek flowing serenely beyond.

Mother and I had been nineteen days on our way from Fairbanks. I'd had a wonderful time — but, as Mother said, I was not old enough to worry about the dangers and the expense, so I could enjoy myself.

First Winter

Mother and I gathered armfuls of dried grass to spread over the slats of the pole beds. We lived with just the basic necessities; there was no money for extras. Food, clothing, household goods and tools had to be packed into Livengood at twenty-five cents a pound.

Fortunately meat was plentiful, and Jack kept the cache supplied with fresh moose meat, rabbits and ptarmigan.

Near the cabin was some open ground which Dad let me stake. I was pretty proud of that. Toward spring Dad and his partners sank several prospect holes on my claim but, like the rest of the creek, it proved to be too low-grade to mine.

My prized possession was a small boxlike phonograph that played cylinder records. It was the only one of that type I ever saw and it was obsolete even in 1915. Mother and I were the only women on the creek for the first six months, and I was the only young girl in the entire country. As a result we had male visitors every few days, including young George and his partner, Albert, who lived a mile up the creek. Several times a week the gang would gather at our cabin to spend the evening. Five Hundred was a popular card game at the time, but I was never allowed to play it. Dad had the idea that girls should not play cards.

Once a month we received mail by pack horse. We paid twenty-five cents a letter, but oh, were we glad to get them! There was no school at the camp, and very little reading material. Every scrap of print that I could lay my hands on, I read and re-read until it wore out. We had packed our dishes with pages from the *Comfort Magazine* for cushioning. We didn't realize how precious those pages were until we pasted them to the logs to keep the moss and bark from dropping onto our food. When I got lonesome I would stand on a box and read the pages. Of course, the most interesting part was always pasted face down on the logs.

The winter wore on. A lot of prospect holes were put to bedrock. Some holes they panned were so promising, the gang felt sure there was a paystreak if only they could find it. Young George was one of the most ambitious prospectors on the creek. He had a large holding of claims which looked so rich that he was offered twenty-five thousand dollars for them, but he refused — a decision he regretted ever after.

George and his partner, Albert, had a good prospecting outfit which included a boiler, hoist, cables, points and pipes. The points were hollow pipes in various lengths, used to thaw the frozen earth when sinking prospect holes or a mine shaft. The point was driven into the frozen ground with a large hammer. Pipe or hose connected the point with the boiler, and through this line steam was forced into the point to thaw the ground.

The experienced prospector, taking all the angles into consideration, could thaw a hole almost the exact size he wanted. The object was to reach bedrock and pan the gravel directly above it to see whether it contained enough gold to justify setting up a mining plant. The smaller the volume of dirt handled on the way down, the less backbreaking labor, and the faster the progress.

All through the winter and early spring George and Albert worked day and night. By May of 1916 their eighty-foot shaft was within a thaw or two of bedrock. It was Albert's turn to work in the hole. He had been down only a few minutes when he rang two bells, the signal to be hoisted up. George began bringing him up, but before Albert reached the top he was overcome by gas and fell out of the sling to the bottom of the hole.

I will never forget that morning when George came running to our cabin for help. Dad and his partner ran back with him, and Mother and I followed. The gas was too strong for anyone to go down in the shaft. The men worked for hours putting down a hose to force fresh air into the shaft and drive out the gas. To test the air they lighted a candle, but the candle went out immediately. Several times one man or another attempted a descent, tied securely in the sling, but the gas drove them back.

Early in the afternoon the men agreed there was no chance Albert was still alive. They could only wait for the gas to clear so they could bring out the body. George was so broken up he could hardly speak. I wanted very much to put my arm around him to comfort him, but that would have been improper so I didn't.

Later that day they brought up the body. Wrapped in a blanket and tied to a pack horse, Albert was taken to Livengood to be buried. He rests on the hillside above town with other early pioneers of the camp.

Back to School

Because there was no school in Livengood, my mother and step-father arranged for me to live in Fairbanks. Our friends Jess and Clara Rust had room for me, and I would help take care of their two young daughters. Best of all, my closest friend, Margaret Gillette, lived next door to the Rusts. For a whole year I had seen no one my age. I could hardly wait to return to school and be with friends.

In late August, 1916, I boarded the stage in Livengood for the three-day trip to Olnes. The stage was a large, heavy wagon pulled by four horses. The road wound along the hillside strewn with heavy boulders and tree stumps, and cut through the valley in axle-deep mud. It was a good day if we covered twenty miles. After staying overnight at a roadhouse, we rose at six, ate breakfast, and began wrenching and rocking over the rough road. The hard plank seats didn't help, either. At Olnes, fifteen miles from Fairbanks, I gratefully boarded the narrow-gauge railroad and traveled the rest of the way in comfort.

To be back in school with all my friends was wonderful, though having missed so much, I really had to work hard to keep up with the eighth-grade class.

Teacher was in the midst of a romance that winter and was very touchy about it. Any mention of her boyfriend really ruffled her feathers. One classmate, a natural-born comic and quite an artist, drew a weekly comic strip on the progress of her romance. These were slyly passed from hand to hand, until a few of those drawings fell into teacher's hands, and we were all punished.

Uncle Jim must have known how broke my parents were that year. Every few weeks he sent me a newsy letter and enclosed a five dollar bill. His kindness provided me with enough money for a movie and the few personal items I needed. At times I was painfully aware of the monotony of my wardrobe, which consisted of three home-made dresses, although I did have a nice store-bought coat which sort of evened things out.

The Rusts were kind and jolly and I enjoyed helping with their two little girls. All too soon school was over. It was spring and time I returned to Livengood. I wanted to stay in Fairbanks, but Mother was not well and I was needed.

Mother and Dad came to meet me when I arrived in Livengood. Standing with them was young George, dressed in a new blue overall suit with a big smile on his face. After my folks greeted me, George came forward shyly to shake my hand, and held it a bit longer and a bit tighter than necessary. I hadn't suspected that he liked me well enough to take a twelve-mile hike just to say hello. I began to ponder about this thing called love.

Since no paystreak had been found on Mike Hess Creek, Dad and his partner moved their operation to Amy Creek where bedrock was only fifteen feet from grassroots. The showing of gold dust in the prospect holes was so encouraging that they decided to try a season of open-cut mining. Before the spring thaw my folks had moved by dog team to a two-room log cabin halfway up the hill on Amy Creek. The rest of the camp — cookhouse and bunkhouse — constructed of tent, pole and rough boards, was strung out between our cabin and the works near the creek.

Mother had six men to cook for, and my job was to set and clear the table and wash the dishes. I also learned to cook, and began baking bread for several of the bachelor outfits nearby. Baking bread was a problem for most of the bachelor prospectors and they considered themselves lucky if they could get a woman to bake for them.

This is how it worked: the men brought over a fifty-pound sack of flour and a can of shortening, told me how many loaves of bread they needed for the week, and we decided which day they could pick up the bread. Some of the men hiked several miles after a day's work, to call for their bread and carry it home in a clean flour sack. They paid me five dollars for baking fifty pounds of flour.

As soon as George discovered that I was baking bread, he asked me to bake for his outfit. This gave him a good reason for coming over once a week and spending the evening. Week by week we became better acquainted. I found myself counting the days until his next visit. Though he had not so much as offered to hold my hand, I was well aware of his love for me.

Belle of the Bush

During those early years in Livengood there were about fifty men to every woman. Being the only young, unmarried girl in the entire camp, I could have had many beaux if I had given them any encouragement. A number of young men — and older ones, too — came around and tried to make up to me, but I was not interested.

Billy was the most determined. "You'll marry me eventually," he insisted. "Just to prove how sure I am, I'm sending to Fairbanks for the best set of silverware in town and I'll have it engraved with your initials and mine."

"Please, Billy, save your heart and your silverware for some other girl. I'll never marry you," I told him.

"We'll see about that," Billy said. "I'll bring the silverware as soon as it comes."

He stopped by the cabin once a week for the next several months. Then one afternoon he arrived with a large package which he handed me. "Here's your silverware," he said. "Open it and take a look."

I handed it back. "I told you I didn't want it," I said.

After a few minutes of arguing his temper began to show. He picked up his package. "I'll be back," he said and slammed the door. He did return many times. My mind remained unchanged, but my curiosity has bothered me ever since. Did the silverware really have his initials and mine on it? Was it as lovely as Billy claimed? I'll never know.

Even though I could not accept their proposals, those young men did cheer my heart on those dull, dark winter days when there was nothing to do but cook and clean and do the laundry on a washboard. It took dozens of trips to the snowbank to fill the tub on the back of the stove to get enough wash water. The clothes were wrung out by hand and hung to dry on lines across one end of the cabin.

On rare occasions we would hike to Livengood and stay with friends for a day or two. It was a cold day in midwinter when George walked me home from town. That meant an extra ten-mile hike for him. It was twenty below, on an old wood road beside a five-foot snowbank, when he asked me to marry him. It was too cold for him to hold my hand, or even stop long enough to put his arm around me. Family life in a log cabin left little chance for private conversations. Here in the vast, white stillness there was no one to overhear words meant only for one.

Ever since the day we'd tallied the freight as it came off the barge at Logjam, my heart had sort of leaned in George's direction. I admired everything about him — his honesty, sincerity, his shy, sometimes awkward efforts to please, his clean-cut appearance, nice gray eyes and wavy black hair. My heart cried: "Yes!" but my mind said, "Be absolutely sure before you promise."

"Would you mind if I thought it over for a few weeks?" I asked. "The way I feel about you must be love, but I intend to be absolutely sure. A good and lasting marriage is the one thing I want most out of life, so I must be very careful."

"Take all the time you need, my dear," he said. "I want you to be absolutely sure. I want you for a lifetime."

A month later I told my folks that we were engaged. It came as no surprise to Mother or Dad.

Getting Married

I was seventeen when George and I became engaged. I set the wedding date for late summer and took a cook's job at a nearby mining camp.

Mother did not approve of my working away from home, but the thought of having money of my own was very appealing. By fall I should have enough money for a pretty dress.

The mess hall where I lived and worked was a one-room cabin with a huge wood-burning stove. I eyed it with a tinge of terror, a monster to be tamed. Under the small window was a long table covered with oilcloth. A shelf beneath held the tools of the trade — pots and pans of every size, stacked helter-skelter.

On the opposite wall were shelves for dishes and spices, and on the floor were cases of canned goods, dried fruit, macaroni, spaghetti, and sacks of flour, sugar, dried beans and peas. My bunk was in the corner. I had a milk case for my wash stand, and several nails driven into the logs for my "closet." I hung burlap curtains on a wire to enclose my so-called room.

The dining table was a crude affair of two-by-fours and boards covered with white oilcloth. A long wooden bench on each side served as seats. The dishes were white enamelware. Coal oil for the lanterns came in five-gallon cans and, believe me, those empty cans were put to many uses — as water pails, bread boxes and cookie containers. By splitting a can down the center of one side and cutting back to each corner we made small tubs — just the thing for a sponge bath or to soak a pair of tired feet.

Fresh water for the mess hall was packed to the camp twice a day from the nearby creek. A wooden yoke, hand-carved to fit the neck and shoulders, with a rope and hook on each side, was used for this job. Each hook was looped over the handle of a five-gallon can. A short distance from the cabin, in the shade of some trees, was the cache.

With all that food at my disposal, it was my job to get three big meals a day on the table, wash the dishes, and keep the mess hall clean. I'm sure my cooking was not all it should have been, but the men ate everything without complaint. It must have been an improvement over what they had been cooking for themselves.

My wedding was not the kind young girls dream of — no church, no preacher, no white wedding dress and veil. From a traveling salesman who visited camp, I had purchased a gown of pale blue embroidered net. It was high-waisted, with a satin cummerbund and a skirt that touched my toes.

Several days before the wedding, George walked six miles to Livengood to ask the commissioner to come up the creek and perform the marriage service. On his return trip, George stopped at every camp to invite all the "boys" to the wedding. There was only one married couple between our place and town and they agreed to stand up for us. The hour was set for midafternoon. With all the wedding guests, our cabin was so crowded we could hardly move. At the same time, Mother was preparing a roast chicken dinner.

When it came time to exchange our vows we stood in the front yard — a small sunlit hillside with Mother's flower beds scattered here and there among the rocks, wildflowers and weeds. George and I stood hand in hand, joining our lives together with all the faith in the world, faith in ourselves and faith in each other. Our old phonograph provided background music, except that midway through the record got stuck on "Flow gently, sweet Afton, a-mang thy green braes," and then, "hik," as the needle hit the crack and flipped back to "Flow gently, sweet Afton. . . ."

After all the good wishes and hand-shaking, Mother dried her tears and served a fine dinner. Later that evening George and I changed from our wedding finery to our old clothes and hiked six miles down the creek to our new home. During the summer George had bought a house for us in Livengood. It cost three hundred dollars and was only one room, but it had real wallpaper on the walls, linoleum on the floor, and two nice windows. I was pleased with the small wood-burning cook stove, the homemade table, and the three store-bought chairs, including a rocker. The double bed had a white iron bedstead with real springs and a mattress. This was pretty fancy compared to the pole bunk with dried grass mattress I was used to.

My young husband was off to his mining job each morning with a lunch in his pocket. He returned at six each evening. I kept the cabin spic and span, cooked the meals, and did the washing on a board. George and I were the youngest couple in the country. The old-timers took a personal interest in the newlyweds. Some made bets as to how long it would be before the bride went home to Mother.

Family Life

In the fall of 1919, I went to Fairbanks to stay with Jess and Clara Rust and await the birth of our first child, a son born in the Rust house in the early morning of August 18. We named him Jess.

The following year we sold our little house in Livengood and moved up the creek, where George sank prospect holes all summer with disappointing results. If all those holes were laid end to end, the tunnel would reach halfway to China! Later George went into partnership on another claim and we moved again. It was my job to take care of the baby, the house and my husband, and cook for a crew of six men.

In the summer of 1921 I was expecting my second child, and I planned to have it on the creek, without a doctor or nurse. Mother agreed to help me when my time came. Very early on the day of the baby's birth, she set out for our cabin. It was a six-mile hike, and Mother arrived at the very moment I was sending for her.

Things got pretty rough. I do remember George sitting beside the bed holding my hand. The sweat gathered on his pale face in large beads, and ran down his cheeks, and dripped on his shirt. Two-year-old Jess was supposed to be sleeping in his homemade bed in the tent room, but he was jumping up and down hollering, "I want Mama." We made it through the night, and by morning the new baby, a plump nine-pound girl, was born with a head of heavy black hair that looked like a windblown bob. We named her Betty.

George left the mining operation and we moved back into Livengood, where he could find a steady job. By this time the camp had simmered down to a few hundred people. We were like one big family with our petty squabbles and arguments, yet if one was sick or in trouble, the entire camp came forth to help. That winter the flu struck. In just a few days nearly everyone had a high fever. When the worst was over there were five new graves on the hillside behind town.

In the spring we moved again, to a rough log cabin halfway up a steep hillside on Kobish Gulch, where George was engaged in another mining project. The back end of the house was dug into the hill and the front end was up on a dirt-filled pole cribbing four feet high. I never dared let the children out the door alone for fear they would fall off the cribbing and roll down the hill into the large ditch at the bottom.

I cared for the two babies, cooked for seven men and did all our laundry on a washboard. Dad's camp was three miles away, down the hill, across the valley, and halfway up the hill on the other side. Mother tried to visit once a week, but she didn't always make it.

It had not rained all summer and the country was drying up. The men had no water to sluice, and there was very little to drink. Fires started in the thick timber on the hillsides. Day by day the burning areas increased. At dusk we watched the flames leap from tree to tree on the hillside a mile away. The air was thick with smoke and the sun itself was like a red-hot coal of fire. The smoke burned our eyes and noses; we couldn't see the boiler house a short distance away.

After the fire a strange thing happened. Our water supply began to increase even though it hadn't rained. Every day the water in the creek rose until there was a good-sized stream. The ditch filled up and again there was water for sluicing — all this without a drop of rain. The burning moss had melted acres of permafrost. The water that flowed into the stream had probably been in cold storage for hundreds of years.

When Jess was kindergarten age we decided to move to Fairbanks so he could attend school. That summer a young flier began making weekly trips to Livengood from Fairbanks in his small single-engine plane. Aeroplanes were something new in Alaska in 1924. I had never been close to one and I was scared of it, but when I considered that a trip overland by wagon would take five days and the flight took three hours, I decided to take the chance.

The plane was a small, open affair, built to carry one adult passenger and the pilot. The round openings, one behind the other in the fuselage, were where the passenger and pilot rode. I wedged myself, feet first, down the hole and put Jess beside me and three-year-old Betty on my lap. As I waved goodbye to Mother and George my heart sank to my socks, but it was too late to back out.

We were head and shoulders above the fuselage, right behind the motor and propeller. When the rush of the wind from the propeller hit us in the face, we gasped like fish out of water. The roar of the engine was terrifying. Jess was so scared he just froze and stayed frozen the entire trip, without blinking an eye. Betty tried to climb out of the plane and could have done so easily if I hadn't held onto her. She fought like a little wildcat until I pushed her down between my knees and held her there with both hands until she exhausted herself and went to sleep.

It was certainly a different mode of transportation from the way I had entered the Livengood country nearly ten years earlier.

Home In Fairbanks

We rented a house in Fairbanks for twelve dollars and fifty cents per month. George thought that sum was wasteful, so he found a four-room log house which we bought for one hundred seventy-five dollars. It was partly furnished, and it had carpeting in the big bedroom and oilcloth on the kitchen walls.

George went to work as a carpenter. He soon learned all the old-timers could teach him, then he sent for a correspondence course in carpentry, and for the next few years he devoted all his spare time to study. I'll never forget the first three hundred dollars he brought home for his month's wages. We were both so proud we nearly burst. When our savings reached the thousand-dollar mark, we splurged and bought me a fur coat (muskrat, one hundred fifty dollars), and George a car — a second-hand Chevrolet for three hundred fifty dollars.

In 1927 our third child was born at home, another boy, whom we named Karl. Some time later, Mother and Dad moved into town and bought a log cabin not far from us. One spring when the ice jammed up on Leo bar, our house flooded and we had to move out for several weeks until the water receded. A couple of years later the river overran its banks and flooded our house again. It was heartbreaking to go in there and clean up the mess the second time. We decided it was time to buy a lot on higher ground and build our own house.

We aimed high. This time we would have a real home. It would have a bathroom with a flush toilet, plenty of windows, lots of closet space, three large bedrooms and hardwood floors. George drew up the plans and we spent the winter remodeling, rearranging, revising and changing, all on paper.

In the spring of 1931 we bought a lot at Eighth and Kellum, across the street from Jess and Clara Rust, for one hundred twenty-five dollars. At that time the wooden courthouse was being torn down to make way for the concrete building which now stands at Second and Cushman. The used lumber was offered for sale. George bought it, and while he worked on the foundation for our house, the children and I pulled nails out of the lumber and sorted it.

That was certainly a rugged year for all of us. George was working night and day between his job and the house-building. Mother was slowly dying of cancer. For nine long months we watched her become paler and smaller, and there was nothing we could do except make her as comfortable as possible.

Dad was with her evenings, but during the day I tried to keep both cabins going, take care of Mother, keep track of the children, do the laundry for both places, and stay cheerful so I wouldn't worry Mother. I hung onto myself by sheer determination. Mother and I had always been such pals, it didn't seem as if the world could go on without her. Her death in the fall was a crushing blow, even though we had been expecting it for months. Poor little Mother! She was too good and too timid for this world, and her path through life had been a rough and rocky one.

Every evening and every weekend we worked on the house. Occasionally George hired a man to assist him with things he was unable to do alone, but for the most part he built the house single-handed except for the help of the children and me. When winter came the house was enclosed, with a stove for heat, which enabled us to do the inside work. In June of 1932 we moved in. The house had a full basement, and it was a story-and-a-half with seven rooms and a bath. We had hardwood floors, a bathroom and sixteen windows!

By that time we had exhausted our savings and owed a twelve hundred dollar mortgage, but it was worth it. I had moved so many times, and never had a real home before. I said to myself, "I'll live in this house until I die!" but it was a promise I could not keep.

Life in the new house was happy and contented. It took several years before all the finishing work was done — the closets, the painting, the wallpaper, the linoleums, but we did it all, George and I.

George was now in the contracting business and the three children were in school. When spring came the children and I planted the entire backyard in vegetables. At the side of the house we set out rhubarb plants and a large strawberry bed. We took a wheelbarrow and went to the woods for birch trees, shrubs and wildflowers to landscape the front yard. When the vegetables were harvested we canned some and stored the rest in the root cellar George had built in the basement. The surplus cabbage became a big keg of sauerkraut.

Two years after we moved into our house one of George's old friends, a former mining partner, died and left us his Livengood mining claims. We sold the claims for a few thousand dollars, which enabled us to pay off the house mortgage and put a few dollars in the bank. We were free from debt. We had running water and a furnace in the basement too.

Our pioneer days were behind us.

*　*　*

That five-year-old girl who came to Fairbanks in 1906 never left Alaska. She and George Bachner lived in their dream home, 1915 Eighth Avenue in Fairbanks, for eight years. Then George took a job as a superintendent with the Morrison Knudsen Company — not bad for a man who'd learned carpentry by correspondence — and they moved to Anchorage. George died there in 1960.

"He was a wonderful person and a wonderful husband," Cleora

said, looking back many years later. "We both worked at our marriage, and got along beautifully for forty-two years."

A year after George's death Cleora married Arne Erickson, also a construction superintendent and a long-time family friend. In 1974 they moved to the Pioneer Home in Fairbanks, where Arne died four years later.

Cleora's older son, Jess, stayed in Fairbanks, where he operates his own flying service. Her daughter, Betty Bachner Chambers, and Karl, in real estate, both live in Anchorage.

On the walls of Cleora's room in the Pioneer Home there were framed pictures of her children, grandchildren and great-grandchildren, and one of her with her step-brother, Adolph, standing in Noyes Slough with their pet dogs, in 1907. That was the year her parents were divorced and Adolph went, reluctantly, with his father. Six years later Cleora heard from him.

"We were on Mike Hess Creek," she said, "and he was in Gardiner, Oregon. He'd had a very hard life with our father, and he ran away when he was sixteen. He was working in a logging camp, he liked his job, and he'd saved a hundred dollars. That was a lot of money in 1916!

"We exchanged a number of letters that winter, then his stopped coming and mine came back marked 'Person Unknown.' I wrote directly to the man I'd been writing in care of — Joseph — I can't remember his last name — and got a curt reply. He said he had never heard of an Adolph Casady. I wrote to the postmaster in Gardiner. He replied that there never had been anyone by my brother's name in the town, and advised me to drop the matter. I had no choice. I was too young and we were too poor to investigate.

"For years I hoped he would write again, or come to Fairbanks, but he never did. I suspect he was killed in the logging camp, and the fact was hushed up. I never heard from my father."

There were no pictures of either George or Arne in Cleora's room. "Their faces are engraved on my heart," she said. "I need no reminders."

Cleora led a quiet life those last years, rarely leaving her room and then in a motorized wheelchair. Her round blue eyes, shining in a frame of snow-white hair, still served her well and she never lost her love of reading. Shortly before her death [September, 1984], looking back over her seventy-five years in the North, she said, "They were good years. Alaska has given me everything I ever wanted."

134

AN EMPIRE-BUILDER
and
AN INDEPENDENT WOMAN

Martin Harrais

The accounts in this section are based on autobiograhical writings of Martin Harrais and Margaret Keenan, found in the University of Alaska Archives, Fairbanks.

L et us now consider the man Martin Harrais — Russian immigrant, sailor, scholar, miner, founder of Chena, and dreamer of empire-buiding.

Born in Latvia in 1865, he ran away from home when he was nine. He took to the sea, and endured a sailor's hardships until he was eighteen. Harrais came ashore on the Pacific Coast, eager to claim America's promise of freedom and opportunity. Even as an immigrant — homeless, friendless, dollarless — he knew he could achieve that dream.

He worked in the Seattle shipyards by day and went to night school to learn English. In his pocket he carried a child's reader and spelling book to add to his vocabulary. Later he took high-school classes at the YMCA until he was ready to enter the University of Washington. During the five years he attended college he worked nights, lived on fifteen dollars a month, and found time to sing in the male quartet, serve as student body president, play football, and graduate with honors.

In 1897 he received his degree, and was offered a position to teach geology at the university. He was thirty-two. It took him ten seconds to say no. He wrote, "Who wanted to teach geology — theorizing over imaginary deposits while the real deposits of gold were up North, waiting for anyone who had the red blood to go in and take them."

Besides, Harrais had in his pocket a letter from Thomas Lippy, who had gone into Dawson with his wife in 1896. He wrote to Martin, "For a young man who can rough it, this is the country to come to."

Martin said yes to that in less than ten seconds. He left Seattle with several partners in the spring of 1897, a full year ahead of the great stampede. Harrais wrote:

Martin Harrais, runaway immigrant, sailor, scholar, turned down a university teaching job in 1897 to seek fortune in the North.

We landed in front of the town [Dawson] on the afternoon of August 12. About a dozen men came down and hailed us with a friendly greeting. Some wanted to know if we had anything to sell, especially fresh potatoes, for which they offered a dollar a pound. That was an eye-opener. In Seattle, we could buy a ton of potatoes for ten dollars. Here we were offered two hundred times that! It was a breathtaking introduction to the new land. Others asked us to go to work for them at once, offering fifteen dollars a day. In Seattle, if one were fortunate enough to have a job, he worked for thirty dollars a month.

While we were talking . . . a man in front of the saloon called, "Come on boys, and have a drink with me." His invitation included everyone on the street and waterfront. Our party were all temperance men and we were reluctant to go, but the camp host was so insistent that we joined the crowd in the bar. John Lee, an Eldorado King, had just arrived in town with his latest cleanup. His poke was lying on the bar. "Go ahead," Lee said, "feel it." I picked up the poke, ran my fingertips over the pebbly sides, then took out a handful of gold and let it run slowly from one hand to the other. Gold — virgin nugget gold — thirty-two pounds of it!

I later owned many such pokes of gold, but they never had quite the same significance to me as that first one. "What will be your pleasure?" the barman asked. "Lemonade," I answered, to the amazement of our host and the whole crowd. Lemonade was not to be had, so we took cigars. After the first round, "Let's have another, boys. There's lots more gold where this came from." And there was — between seventy-five and a hundred tons of it on Eldorado alone.

It took three days to pitch our tent and build a cache in which to store our goods. The cache was a necessity, not as a protection from our fellowmen — there was no means of locking it, and none was needed — but from the elements. We cut our boat in half, hoisted it on eight-foot posts out of reach of male-mute dogs, used one half for the body, and the other half for the roof. We stored our food within, hung a canvas over the opening and called it finished.

On the fourth day we took our packs on our backs, including food, cooking utensils and bedding, and went to take our first look at the creeks where there was "lots more where this came from." The first night we camped on No. 27 Bonanza Creek. Frank Smith of our party was acquainted with the owner, and we were welcomed with extra warmth.

During the three months on the trail to Dawson, each of us had determined in his own mind the stake with which he would be content to return to the States and engage in some business or profession. Mine was ten thousand dollars. That evening on the creek something happened to the dollar goal that had seemed ample. Our host invited us to go with him the next morning to Billy Chappell's cleanup on Eldorado.

Billy's claim was one of the few shallow places where mining was carried on that summer by the open-cut method. The cleanup work was already done, and several neighbors were gathered around two gold pans full of gold, lying in the open pit. They were hefting the pans and guessing the value of the gold — each pan was worth more than six hundred dollars. No envy was expressed in any manner; everyone was glad Billy had struck it; everyone was sure his own claim was as good as, if not better than, Billy's. Our cheechako eyes were bulging with admiration. There was self-congratulation that we, too, could go and do likewise.

It is true that we were driven to Alaska to escape the panic that prevailed in the States. There were labor strikes; Kansas and Nebraska farmers were burning corn for fuel; jobs were not to be had on Puget Sound. The only choice was to join Coxey's army of unemployed and march to Washington, D.C. — or go North. We were sane men and women, above the average in intelligence and energy. The timid ones never started to Alaska, and the weak ones died on the way. We came to this wilderness to better our conditions of life. It never occurred to us to ask for either government or private assistance.

The first winter in Dawson Harrais shared a crude log cabin with his partners. It had a dirt floor and oiled flour sacks for windowpanes. While the other men had pictures of their families and loved ones, Martin had none. His personal possessions included a Bible and the complete works of Shakespeare. By the light of the lamp — a bowl of bacon grease with moss for a wick — he read both books from cover to cover.

One of the first jobs Harrais had in Dawson was a contract to whipsaw four thousand feet of sluice-box lumber for Alex MacDonald, Klondike King. Martin and his partner finished the sawing in twenty days, and received twelve hundred eighty dollars in gold dust.

Martin Harrais was seeking — and finding — his fortune.

Railroad-Builder

M artin Harrais struck it rich in the Klondike. For seven years he worked claims on Bonanza and All Gold creeks. He was a millionaire when he left Dawson in the late fall of 1903 for the strike in the Tanana Valley of Alaska — one thousand miles by dog team. This was not a will-o-the-wisp venture. Harrais, at thirty-eight, was too practical for that. He had a purpose, and his partner, Falcon Joslin, had a vision. Joslin, a lawyer who had built a light plant, opened a coal mine, and built a narrow-gauge railroad in Dawson, wanted to build a railroad from a point on the Tanana River to connect river transportation with the new mining camps on Pedro, Cleary and Gilmore creeks.

Word of the Felix Pedro strike was out, but the big rush was yet to come. Once again Martin was head of the pack. He wrote:

> We spent several weeks in our investigation and decided to build the railroad. We selected Chena, at the head of navigation for large riverboats, as the terminal. The name was properly Chenoa, but the printer publishing the weekly newspaper was short one "O" for setting up the headline, so he set it up "Chena" instead and the name was written thus into government records.
>
> From Chena we ran the location line twenty-one miles to Gilmore in the dead of the first winter. We secured brown wrapping paper, platted our survey line, and rolled it up. Frank Smith carried it back to Falcon Joslin in Dawson with our compliments — the opening act in our dream of empire-building in the North.
>
> In the latter part of winter I located mining ground on Goldstream. As there were no boilers or steam plants to be had in the country, and the winter season was far too advanced to sink holes with wood fires, I did not do any development work on the ground. However, there was a shortage of lumber for sluice boxes for the spring cleanup, so I assembled enough machinery — a boiler out of a small riverboat, an engine, and a saw and carriage — to build a sawmill in Chena that winter. I used it to cut sluice lumber for creek use.
>
> In the spring and summer of 1904, the Fairbanks stampede was in full swing. It was a repetition of Dawson and Nome days, except there were no cheechakoes. If any came, they were so quickly absorbed that no one noticed them.

The stampeders brought their mining plants from both Dawson and Nome. They proceeded to look the creeks over, get a lay on some of the ground, put their plants on it, and go to work. There were few shallow places in the Fairbanks mining area — most of it was digging — but we brought our mining experience, machinery and capital. The development was rapid. By midsummer the miners were taking gold out by the ton. Consequently, I could send a good report to Falcon Joslin, who had gone Outside to promote a railroad for this district.

Falcon succeeded in interesting the White Pass and Yukon Railroad Company in our project. It was reported that the White Pass Railroad from Skagway to Whitehorse on the Yukon River paid for itself the first year in operation. As a result, the company was optimistic about Alaska.

Joslin and Harrais had done their homework. At the time they proposed the railroad, freighters with sleds and horse-drawn wagons charged one to ten dollars a ton-mile for hauling goods from Fairbanks to the camps. The higher rate was in effect when trail conditions were bad, which was the rule rather than the exception. The railroad, to be named the Tanana Valley Railroad (TVRR), would charge a standard eighty-six cents per ton-mile and corner the market.

With the financial backing of New York and Chicago businessmen, Joslin launched the TVRR for a cost of five hundred thousand dollars. The first boatload of construction material was shipped in the fall of 1904, but unfortunately the boat was caught in the freeze-up sixty miles downriver — and Harrais had to dispatch dog teams to haul the supplies to Chena over the river ice. That was the first of many difficulties to plague the ambitious undertaking.

On April 4, 1905, Joslin, president of the new railroad, arrived in Chena with Charles Moriarity, superintendent of construction; Robert Taylor, accountant; and Adam Tyson, general storekeeper. Later came transit man John Bernard, treasurer L.L. James, and two timekeepers. "That was the overhead force during the construction days — eight men," Harrais said. "My part was to finance the project until Outside capital was enlisted, and to furnish lumber."

The lumber was no small item. Native spruce was used for the

The Tanana Valley Railroad, financed by Harrais' mining wealth, was to be the first link in a vast railroad network in Alaska.

ties and trestles. In some places, trestles six hundred feet long were required to bridge the creeks. Lumber was needed for four station houses, roundhouses and shops.

All the rails and heavy equipment were shipped six thousand miles and handled as many as eleven times. At the peak of construction — under the able hand of Jim Hall, who was trained on the Great Northern and White Pass railroads — two hundred men worked on the railroad and completed a total of twenty-six miles of narrow gauge the first year from Chena to Gilmore with a 4.7-mile spur to Fairbanks. Laborers received seven dollars and fifty cents per day.

By late September, 1905, the TVRR was rolling trains on the line daily. The following summer the railroad was extended twenty miles to Chatanika. Equipment included four locomotives, four passenger coaches, and thirty-eight freight cars. The commuter train between Fairbanks and Chena, which ran twice a day, took forty-five minutes. The "Goldstream Special," which started at Chatanika, picked up passengers at Olnes, Ridgetop, Gilmore, Fox, Eldorado, Ester Siding and Chena Junction, to arrive in Fairbanks four and one-half hours later.

In those days Fox had a population of five hundred; Gilmore and Olnes, three hundred each, and Chatanika, six hundred fifty. Fairbanks, the little Klondike of the Far North, had a population of five thousand.

Joslin and Harrais had high hopes for the TVRR. They saw it as the first link in a vast network of railroads in Alaska. Even before the TVRR was completed, they spoke about an extension to Circle City and a six-hundred-mile link to Nome. They envisioned another set of rails up the Tanana Valley and across the Yukon boundary to Lynn Canal, to link the Interior to the waterways. On board would be a wonderful wealth of gold, copper, silver, oil and lead that had already been discovered. That was just the beginning.

It was really the end. Federal regulation stifled and finally snuffed out mineral development. Then, by presidential edict in 1906, President Theodore Roosevelt withdrew all Alaska coal, oil and timberlands to reserve them for future generations. He acted at the urging of coal and timber barons in the States, who feared competition from Alaska — and the dreams of an empire-builder.

In 1909 the golden years in Fairbanks and Chena were over.

Miss Keenan

While Martin was struggling to build an empire on the shifting sands in the Territory of Alaska, Margaret Keenan was superintendent of schools for Custer County, Idaho, a position she held for five years. Custer County was less developed than Fairbanks — no railroads, telephones or telegraph. Miss Keenan traveled her district on horseback.

"When I came out of Idaho I had learned, through sheer necessity, to ride like a cowboy, and shoot a rattlesnake through the neck in one shot with a six-shooter," Margaret wrote in her unpublished autobiography.

The job was one with many challenges for a young woman at the turn of the century. Keenan went about it with a great show of confidence, even though there were many times she was tempted to go back home to the security of her family. But Miss Keenan had not descended from quitters.

Born of pioneer stock in Batesville, Ohio, in 1872, she grew up on the ideals of liberty her ancestors had expressed when fighting with General Washington in the Revolution, and commanding Old Ironsides. Margaret was the sixth child in a family of seven. She excelled in her studies, taught school immediately upon graduating from high school, and later worked her way through college by tutoring math students. Her degree was from Valparaiso University.

Miss Keenan was blessed with beauty as well as brains. Her complexion was porcelain-white, with a natural blush to her cheeks, and smiling red lips. She had a proud lift to her head and fine, silky auburn hair that, when loosened from its bun, tumbled down her back in soft, natural curls. She was tall and well proportioned — a "perfect 36" cherished in that era. She was fiercely independent, and a woman of incredibly high standards. As president of the Idaho Women's Temperance Union, she took a staunch stand against alcohol.

In Idaho there were eleven unmarried men for every single woman. Naturally one of them asked for her hand in marriage. His name does not once appear among her papers. We do know that shortly after their marriage he opened a bar and liquor store.

"You make the choice," she told her husband. "The bar or me." He said the business was too lucrative to pass up. She divorced him and took back her maiden name.

Miss Keenan first came to Alaska in 1902 with a sister, on a sightseeing trip to Sitka. In 1914 she accepted the position of principal of the Skagway schools. Friends gave her the name of Martin Harrais, who was "up there somewhere — probably near Fairbanks." During the two years Margaret was in Skagway she often heard his name, and she grew curious about this self-made man of the North who had been too busy to take a wife. He was still a bachelor at forty-nine.

In 1916 Margaret moved to Fairbanks to take the job as superintendent of schools — at a salary of two hundred seventy-five dollars a month. She traveled to the Interior by steamboat with a friend who had a letter of introduction to one Martin Harrais of Chena.

"I happened to be in the depths of an after-lunch siesta when we arrived in Chena," Miss Keenan wrote. "My friend went ashore to discover that His Nibs was 'somewhere on the creek.' I have always felt a little hesitancy about presenting letters of introduction. They seem to say so patently 'Well, here I am. What are you going to do about it?' So, in my heart I congratulated His Single Blessedness on his escape from responsibility as host."

But the community did not let her remain in forgetfulness. His name, with "that queer 'ais' ending," was frequently in the news.

"Where did he get that queer name?" she asked a friend.

"I don't know — born somewhere in the Baltic."

"No, Russian."

"A Russian with whiskers and a blouse that he forgets to tuck in?"

"No, he is a graduate of an American university and a gentleman."

To herself she said, "Go softly; this man has friends. It might be worthwhile to pry off his lid and see how his wheels go round."

His lid remained securely in place, however. "For months I was not within speaking distance of him. I saw him at a picture show once and managed to say the wrong thing again. My hostess pointed him out as 'the great Martin Harrais.'

"The one in the middle seat?" I asked. "He would never get my vote in a beauty contest."

"Well, who wants a pretty man?" she responded.

"Not I. I am having too good a time to want any man."

In 1917 Harrais, fifty-two, took an apartment in Fairbanks — across the hall from Miss Keenan, then forty-five and superinten-

Margaret Keenan Harrais and a pupil fish from a skiff near Ellamar. Of her eight Indian pupils she wrote, "They are clean, well-mannered and unbelievably good."

dent of schools. It was inevitable that they meet. When they did, Margaret described Martin this way:

"He is a true Nordic, and looks every inch the part. There is a definite bigness about him that is only partly physical, a bigness of which he is wholly unaware."

Affinity

Harrais, whose fortune had dwindled with the decline of Chena, was still highly respected, but during World War I an ugly rumor started. Martin, who spoke with a Russian accent, was said to be pro-German. When he heard it he was outraged.

"He stalked into my living room that evening with set jaw and eyes as cold and blue as glacier ice," Margaret wrote. "He sat down, fidgeted nervously with his hands, crossed and uncrossed his knees, got up and walked the floor, and sat down again. All this time I was wondering what was the matter with my usually well-poised neighbor."

Finally he blurted out, "Well, I guess I may as well get it off my chest."

Martin told Margaret about the hateful rumor, and why it affected him so deeply. His homeland was Latvia, overrun by Germans who had dispossessed his people of their land and made them serfs. As he explained:

> When the master came down the road, my father had to step to one side with his hat under his arm in servile attention. If the master was ill-humored or drunk, as he frequently was, he reached over and caned my father over the head with his walking stick, and my father had to take it. He had a wife and little children, and there was no place else to go — not a square foot of soil could be acquired by one of his blood. He had to submit to the indignity or his family would starve.
>
> As soon as we children were big enough to be useful, we had to go up to the Mansion House as servants. I, in turn, followed my two sisters, but there was something in my disposition that could not bend the subservient knee. I was constantly in disfavor and was frequently sent home in disgrace. This endangered the welfare of my family. My father would punish me, take me by the hand and lead me back to the Mansion House and apologize for my behavior.

When I was nine, one of my duties was to hold the master's horse when he went out driving. I was the hitching post. I waited outside while the master conducted his business. One cold winter's day I was sent out with the master. He was dressed in rich furs . . . while I had only the little coat of my indoor suit.

My master had several calls to make, but about the middle of the forenoon we came to a tavern where some of his companions were enjoying themselves. He spent the day drinking and gambling while I shivered in the cold and held his horse. Toward evening, a servant brought me a piece of black bread which I shared with the horse.

One of my master's companions looked out the window and reproached my master for his neglect of boy and horse. The party broke up abruptly. The master came out in a black mood, and drove home without a word. I knew he was angry, but I thought he must have lost at cards. When we were inside he flogged me unmercifully because I had humiliated him in the presence of his friends.

I knew I could not take that life any longer, nor could I jeopardize my family's future by rebellion. I went to the dock where a windjammer was ready to sail, and I shipped out with them as a general roustabout. For nine years I suffered harsh, brutal treatment at sea. I was hungry most of the time, friendless, and lonely.

Miss Keenan included Martin's story in her autobiography, "Alaska Periscope." She said of him, "He is the best American I have ever known."

One day during the war Martin stopped at the Red Cross headquarters. His recent mining effort had not turned out well and ready cash was scarce, yet he wanted to do his duty toward the war effort. He took off his handsome overcoat and gave that as his contribution.

"A few more stunts like that," Margaret wrote, "and I'll be foolish enough to marry him in spite of the fact that he is broke. If I marry him, I'll have to speak for myself, since his proposal contained the clause, 'when I'm prosperous again.'

"As far as I'm concerned, it will be when I make up my mind to marry Alaska, too — that's what it means to marry one of these sourdoughs."

During World War I Miss Keenan initiated a Liberty Bond program. Each student bought a fifty dollar war bond with money earned or saved from his personal allowance. She arranged for the bonds to be paid in installments, and she personally underwrote the ten-thousand-dollar debt at the First National Bank.

When the final tally was in, the one hundred eight-six school-children owned more than two hundred Liberty Bonds worth fifty dollars each, and they had enough in thrift stamps to bring the per capita contribution to sixty dollars. No other community in the nation equalled that record.

In 1918 Margaret resigned from her post in Fairbanks, and "reluctantly accepted a position as principal of a high school in Shenandoah, Iowa." She wrote that she would have gladly hitched her star to Martin's wagon, "but I was not invited. He honestly felt that he had nothing to offer me. His courtship reminded me of a letter written by Abraham Lincoln in which he asked the lady of his heart to marry him, but in humility advised her not to do so.

"Martin accompanied me by stage to Chitina. The muscles of my throat tighten yet to think of that last hour waiting for the train — the attempt at casualness, the enforced cheerfulness by which each tried to make the situation a bit easier for the other. I continued Outside while Martin went to work for the Kennecott Copper Corporation near Chitina."

For the next two years Margaret was plagued by influenza and pneumonia, and moved from place to place seeking a better climate for her health — Colorado, Idaho, Portland and finally San Diego, where she took a little house with a big garden. Years later she wrote:

> At this time Martin was up North battling furiously to wrest another fortune to lay at my feet. He felt that he could not honorably ask me to share his lot in life, while I was willing to do just that. Within a year the knowledge that I was ill and among strangers caused Martin to come out and take care of me. We were married at the YMCA in San Diego on October 25, 1920, and no bride ever went home to a mansion more happily than I to our half-pint castle.
>
> My Viking husband promptly deposited to my personal credit the exact price of the home, then rolled up his sleeves and went to work. He added a garage, a chicken house, an improved lawn, and a fine row of shade trees. In five months it was time for him to return to Alaska. I could not yet risk the rigors of the Alaska climate, and his only hope of recouping his fortune was in Alaska. There he had taken out approximately a million dollars in gold, only to lose it in another mining venture. This time he hoped to make — and keep — another stake.

The next two years we spent in much the same fashion, delightful winters in California, and lonely summers apart. At last he found, in the Chitina-McCarthy country, what he considered another good mining property. It was agreed that I would move back to Alaska. I accepted the offer of the McCarthy school board to teach in the fall of 1924. I was joyously on my way back North to a log-cabin home as close to my husband's work as possible. I did not cast one lingering look behind. Home, Love, is where the heart is."

Schoolteacher At McCarthy

Mrs. Martin Harrais arrived in Cordova by boat in the late summer of 1924. There she boarded the Copper River and Northwestern Railroad for a two-day journey into the high country of stunning white glaciers folded within the steep, dark hills. The jagged, snowcapped Wrangell Mountains dwarfed the small settlement of McCarthy, with its squatty cabins, wooden sidewalks and false-fronted saloons. Five miles beyond, perched on the side of a copper mountain, was the Kennecott Copper Mine owned by the Guggenheim Syndicate. Millions of dollars worth of ore had been taken out of the underground tunnels since mining began in 1911.

My husband secured a three-room log cabin which someone had the good taste to build on the very edge of town. It has screened porches at front and back, pantry, wardrobe and built-in shelves. The front porch contains a hammock, a red porch table, and a pile of stove wood.

In the living room is a good sewing machine, a couch piled with more fancy cushions than I ever saw before on one couch, a circular dining table, rocking chairs, a heating stove, and the most remarkable phonograph. It is a combination phonograph with book and record shelves and a library table all in solid mahogany. In the bedroom is a big brass bed, old ivory chiffonier and a three-mirror dressing table. The rose-colored draperies match the coverlet on the bed.

But it is the kitchen that is my delight. It has washable wallpaper in yellow with blue birds flying happily all over it. The furniture is white and fitted as snug as that of a ship's cabin. On the porch is a small barrel for rain water — snow water later — and a water tap. Martin informs me that the tap will soon freeze, and the water will have to be carried from the spring up the canyon. My intrepid little grandmother reared nine children with a spring as the sole source of water supply. There ought to be a little of that same stuff in me.

A pretty white breakfast table stands under the long window, and if I could describe the view from that window I would not be teaching school — I'd be one of the world's great descriptive writers. I have a marvelous view of snowcapped mountains and glaciers, the light and shade of them forever changing. Mount Blackburn, sixteen thousand feet, is framed by the window.

Martin stayed for a week after my arrival, and now is back at his mining. For the first time in my life I am content to sit alone at a table with food in my hands, shifting from straight chair to rocker and back again, trying to read a magazine, anything to dispell the loneliness.

McCarthy was a service center for independent miners like Martin, and a recreation center for the sixteen hundred workers employed at the Kennecott Mine. Everything that was outlawed in the company town — gambling, booze and brothels — was in abundance in McCarthy.

"It is a strange berth in which to find the president of the Territorial Women's Christian Temperance Union," Margaret wrote.

She resumed her work to prevent repeal of Alaska's prohibition law. She received permission from the Territorial Commissioner of Education to send WCTU materials to all one hundred ninety schoolteachers in Alaska. Her stand opposing liquor — when there was an active bootlegging business going on in McCarthy — could not have endeared her to the residents, many of whom earned their living from the illegal traffic.

"Martin thinks I may succeed in teaching out this one year since I have an iron-clad contract," Margaret wrote, "but that I must not expect a renewal of the contract for another year. I accept the challenge.

"The little green and white schoolhouse is amply outfitted. We have the *Encyclopedia Britannica,* a children's library of well-chosen books, and all supplies down to the last sheet of paper. Alaska provides well for her schools. Every year two hundred forty dollars per student is spent for education. There are eleven children in school, nice little things, and there I rest my hope. I never have much hope of reforming middle-aged people, but there are measureless possibilities in the children."

For a number of years all went well, but in the spring of 1930 a great fuss developed over the acceptance of a new member in the Regal Reading Club in McCarthy. One woman, Mrs. Tjoscvig, thought the new member should be ousted. Margaret disagreed. Mrs. Tjosevig wrote to the Commissioner of Education asking that Margaret be relieved of her position because she was an "unfit teacher." Margaret responded to the Commissioner, "Please help preserve the peace for an efficient school year. And now abideth faith, hope and charity — but the greatest of these is a sense of humor." She was retained.

The following year, due to the dwindling population, the school was closed. When copper prices fell from twenty-six cents a pound to four cents, the Kennecott mines curtailed production. Martin continued to pursue an illusive fortune, and Margaret — true to her profession — taught the two remaining McCarthy pupils in her cabin without pay.

Miner's Wife

In the summer of 1931 Margaret was free to be a miner's wife. She left the tidy cabin in McCarthy with its bright, cheerful kitchen and its bedroom with the brass bed, and spent three months with Martin at the mine. It was just the two of them, isolated from the world. About those months she wrote:

> I'm getting pretty good at camp cooking. I can pack into a bag enough food to last five days on the trail. When we arrive at a camping place, I start dinner while Martin unpacks the horses. One can scarcely realize that two people can ride and carry on two horses everything necessary for five days' living in the wilderness — food, dishes, bedding, clothing, tools, gun and mosquito tent — but it can be done. Next spring, when commercial aviation comes to our part of the country, I will fly into the camp. The supplies will still have to be freighted in by trail since twenty-five cents a pound is prohibitive in ton lots.
>
> We have a real garden here at camp with vegetables and flowers, including two rose bushes, to say nothing of our strawberry bed. I carried the plants from McCarthy through deep water and over fallen timber; I cradled them in my arms despite my husband's protest that they were not worth the effort. Not

worth the effort! I have never seen plants grow the way they do in the cleared spot around the camp cabin. The poppies stand straight and regal at eight feet, and the pansies are twenty-two inches tall without support.

I am not a miner, but I can keep busy around the works just the same. I have been calling myself Friday, but my friend Phonograph Sam gave me my true classification. I am a "nipper." Sam explained that in every mine there are men whose business it is to pass tools up to the miners, and such men are called nippers. That is my job exactly. Dressed in knickers and high, laced boots, I tag along with Martin all over the hills and make myself useful.

While he drills holes, I find a safe place to cache the dynamite sack and dig steps around the face of the mountain so we can make a quick getaway after the fuse is lighted. Then I trot back to the cache for the number of sticks of dynamite required for the charge, and stand back. After the shot, it is my job to sort out and pile up the high-grade ore. This may not sound as though it would take much time, but when you have to fight for every foothold on the steep face of the mountain, and climb with both hands and feet, it keeps the nipper as busy as the driller.

Margaret returned to the McCarthy cabin in the fall while Martin stayed at the mine to work until Christmas. He left the camp December 16, headed for home with a fully loaded sled pulled by two horses. It was bitterly cold. The third day out he had to cross the main channel of the Chitina River. He tested the river ice; it was sixteen inches thick. He started across. Midway the horses suddenly dropped through an air hole into deep water. Martin, perched on top of the heavily loaded sled, almost went in behind them.

For two desperate hours Martin cut a channel in the ice in hopes of reaching shallow water so he could lead the horses to safety, but the river was too deep. Then, to his horror, the sled began sliding into the hole. It was forty below, with a bitter wind. One of Martin's feet was wet, and his clothing was covered with ice and snow. Half the sled was under water, but he managed to grab dry clothes and a little food. With that he set out on foot for home — forty miles away.

He got only a little way when he realized there was one gruesome act to be performed. The horses were groaning and writhing in pain from having been in the cold water so long. Martin snatched the sledge hammer from the fast-sinking load and dealt each horse a crushing blow on the forehead — a quick release for the suffering animals, but devasting to the kind-hearted man who loved them.

The short winter day was nearing its close. Neither the wind nor the temperature had moderated. Martin's foot quickly froze. Although desperately weary, he had to keep forging ahead all night to keep his entire body from freezing. He reached a trapper's cabin in the early morning, rested all that day, and hobbled the remaining twenty miles the third day.

"It was after midnight when I heard a strange fumbling at the cabin door," Margaret wrote. "Martin — cold, hungry, haggard from grief and pain — stumbled into my arms. I eased him down to the floor and sprang into action. Food, warmth, comfort, loving assurance — explanations could wait.

"The frozen foot was our deepest concern. We removed the shoepac and sock without further injury. We tried nursing his foot at home, but the condition was too serious for our skill and equipment. Martin tried to minimize the whole affair, but I noted with growing concern the peculiar, sickish odor of gangrenous flesh. Finally, without consulting him, I arranged for a dog team and driver to take him to the Kennecott Hospital where he received expert attention.

"When Martin returned home, he was not able to put his foot on the floor. He got very restless spending time in bed with his foot elevated. Ten weeks is a long time for an active man to lie helpless and grieve over the loss of his beloved horses."

Ellamar

Martin recovered, and the following summer he and Margaret returned to the mine. She went by commercial air service — a forty-minute flight replacing the five grueling days on the trail.

"In comparison, the airplane seemed wonderfully safe, even though we would be the first ones to land on the field, which was handmade without any knowledge of the requirements of our particular aircraft," Margaret wrote.

"I'll admit feeling apprehensive wondering how we were going to land, and that feeling deepened as we circled the field several times. I held my breath. Being all ready for a bump, I was agreeably surprised at the smoothness of the landing, thanks to Harold

Gillam's skill as an aviator. I asked whether it was a successful landing. He replied that any landing you can walk away from is a successful landing, but that he would not land on the field again until the Territory did some work on it."

In 1932 the Harraises left McCarthy for Cordova, where he purchased the Sheep Bay Mill and Lumber Company. He had been hurt financially by the Depression, when several Seattle businesses he had invested in failed, and he lost thirty-five thousand dollars when the copper market dropped.

Finances dictated that Margaret return to teaching. She was forced to take a position at Ellamar, a small coastal settlement of Indians midway between Cordova and Valdez. It as a picturesque spot, and the scene of much copper-mining during World War I. When the mining company ceased operation in 1920 it left behind a townsite with a school and a number of well-built houses, although there was no store nor post office. Margaret lived upstairs over the school. She taught eight Indians, all ages, whom she described as "clean, well-mannered, and unbelievably good." Of her years there she wrote:

> The school property is so close to the Pacific waters that high tide washes over the lower front step. Neither pen nor brush could portray the beauty of the sunset I see before me. The mail boat is due the tenth of every month — if weather permits. If not, it comes when it comes. My daily paper comes in stacks. I read them, then start them round the circle of my neighbors. They travel slowly from home to home, and finally back to me.
>
> The money is good for these troubled times, and I have two furnished rooms for living quarters, plus coal, kindling, kerosene, gasoline and janitor service thrown in. After the hectic experience and upheavals of the past years, this seems a haven of peace and security. How fortunate I am when so many are deprived of the high privilege of working.

Margaret worked at Ellamar for two years. During that time Martin was appointed United States commissioner at Valdez, a position which carried with it the ex-officio title of justice of the peace. He had many duties, but little pay. He bought a six-room house, built by a banker in the early days. Margaret said:

> The house — rather pretentious — is in need of repair, but Martin can handle that. He enjoys building up a place, and

he knows how, so he is as happy as they come in these difficult days.

We have two big lots which are to be fenced and planted with flowers, grass, berries and vegetables. Won't I have a glorious time in that garden! There is no formal exercise that can compete with constructive outdoor activity.

The house is to be redecorated inside and out, so I am studying catalogs and seed books in preparation. There is a complete bathroom, think of it! We will have oil for heating and cooking, supplemented by an electric grill in the kitchen, and electric heaters in the upstairs rooms. No more wood, coal and ashes! There is a vacuum cleaner, electric washer and water pump. Here in Ellamar I pack the snow in a tub, carry it up a steep stairway, melt it, and strain out the dried grass. At the close of this school year I shall go to Valdez to enjoy our new home. I hope this will be my last year of teaching. I have steadfastly contended that we are not poor — we only have no money.

That was not Margaret's last year of teaching. In 1935 she moved to Fort Liscum (later known as Dayville) near Valdez, to teach one last year. She had reached the compulsory retirement age, but asked for — and received — an extension. The reason was money. Martin's salary as commissioner was not enough to buy a house and provide income for their remaining years.

Margaret spent Thanksgiving Day with Martin in their Valdez home. She reluctantly left him to resume her duties at Fort Liscum. A few weeks later Margaret received word that her husband was very ill. Storms and high waves made it impossible for her to cross the bay. When she did reach Valdez, Martin had been taken to the hospital in Seward, where he died on Christmas Day, 1936, before Margaret was able to reach his side.

Margaret lived in the Valdez house alone for twenty-eight years. She carried on her husband's work as deputy commissioner, and spearheaded many community projects. She never stopped helping others. For many years after her husband's passing she continued to set a place for him at the dinner table.

Margaret retired at ninety. The following year, 1964, after Valdez had been devastated by the Good Friday earthquake and tidal wave, she died.

Of Margaret Keenan Harrais it was said, "Her life has been a model of all that is good and decent and constructive."

TRADER ON THE TANANA

William Henry Newton was born in 1872, at Newcastle-on-Tyne in northern England. He was a tall, well-proportioned man with piercing blue eyes, a slightly Roman nose, fair skin and a well-trimmed moustache. His hair was dark, his head bald from forehead to crown as the result of a fever contracted in South Africa.

Newton was somewhat gallant, a bit aristocratic, at all times quite confident in his beliefs, ideas and opinions. He never gambled, never drank and seldom smoked, but his sense of humor was excellent. Even those who didn't like him respected him.

When he was fourteen his mother died. His younger brother and two sisters were able to adjust to their father's new wife and her two sons, but William could not. He finished public school, but then had a terrible quarrel with his father and was disowned.

At seventeen he headed for the diamond mines in South Africa, then to Australia, where he worked on a sheep ranch. When he heard of the Klondike gold strike, he came to the North. By then he was twenty-five. He didn't strike it rich in the Klondike, nor in Nome. That left one more stampede, Fairbanks, but his luck wasn't any better there. He became a commercial hunter and fisherman. He supplied Fairbanks restaurants with fresh-water fishes, game birds, moose, caribou and mountain sheep.

By 1905 he had saved enough money to go into business. He built a trading post on the Tanana River, five miles downstream from Healy Lake. It was a remote location, inhabited by Indians and visited on rare occasions by the few steamboats that managed to get that far upriver. It was a good place for a loner, and there was money to be made in the fur trade. William thrived. He could afford to take a wife.

Through his sisters in England he began corresponding with Jane Hilton Thompson, a schoolteacher, petite and a bit prim but sturdy. She had gray-blue eyes, rich brown hair, an oval face and skin so fair it burned when exposed to the sun. Hers was a large, musical Episcopalian family, and her social life revolved around family, friends, church and village, plays and concerts. She, too, had a quick wit and a good sense of humor.

William and Jane corresponded regularly, and after a suitable time he asked her to be his wife. She agreed to come and meet Newton, but did not promise to stay. She had been frugal during her years of teaching, and the small nest egg she had saved was

William and Jane Newton, transplants from England, prospered at their back-country trading post, but left it to get their three Alaska-born children into formal schools.

her travel fund. She had made one trip, to Paris, before she embarked on a voyage halfway around the world in the spring of 1908.

At Jane's age, thirty-five, her chances for a suitable marriage in England were not good. She wanted a family, and she had a dream — a dream of going to one of the colonies, prospering, and returning to England having done well in the world. Alaska was not one of the colonies, but it would do. She did not expect that her course would be easy. Life had never been easy.

It was summer when Jane stepped off the sternwheeler in Fairbanks. The country was shimmering with green leaves and golden light, and William Newton was there to meet her, handsome in his best suit, displaying his usual confidence and charm. Soon they were married and on their way to William's trading post a hundred and thirty miles southeast of Fairbanks. They traveled ninety miles by horse-drawn wagon over a miserably bumpy road, across creeks, and along hillsides so steep they took Jane's breath away. At the Delta ferry crossing they loaded Jane's belongings into an open riverboat, then left all sign of human habitation behind. Jane was overwhelmed by the vastness of the land, so unlike the compact island she had left behind.

After a forty-mile trip down the Tanana River, the Newtons were home. Home was a log trading post on high, terraced ground overlooking miles and miles of marshes and rolling plains to the snowcapped Alaska Range, misty in the distance.

Trading Post

Two years later their first child, Madge, was born. Then in 1912 Jane had twins — a boy and girl — named Harold and Kathleen. Such a burden would have been the undoing of a lesser woman, but not Jane. She adapted — she did her duty. But three things disturbed her greatly; the plague of gnats and mosquitoes in the summer, the intense cold in the winter, and the isolation all year long. Days, weeks and months went by before she met another woman with whom she could visit. Much of the time she was like an exhausted swimmer, devoting all her energy to survival and submerging her feelings.

The Newtons' trading post and home were all in one log structure, with the store occupying the front half. In the back were the kitchen, living room, two tiny bedrooms and fifty paces beyond the back door — the outhouse.

"I am sure the years on the Tanana would have cost Mother her sanity, had it not been for work, work, and more work," said her son, Hal, who now lives in La Jolla, California. "During the early years she was caring for three babies, baking bread, making clothes, tending the garden, looking after the dogs, and when Dad was away she minded the store."

Indians came to trade their furs for the heavy wool Hudson's Bay blankets, long-handled underwear, pants, shirts, socks, gloves, bandanas, felt hats and calico. William also stocked colored beads for the Native women to do decorative work on leather slippers and mittens. Tobacco was in demand, a strong black leaf that the Indians chewed, and plug tobacco.

"For many years Mother did the laundry in a galvanized tub, on a washboard, with a hand-wringer that clamped to the tub," Hal said. "Of course all the water had to be carried in (and out), and was heated on top of the stove.

"Later she got a primitive paddle washer with an attached hand-wringer. By then we were old enough to push and pull the lever that operated the paddle, and that eased her burden some. She used flatirons with wooden handles, heated on top of the stove. She made most of our clothes — and hers — using a hand-turned table-model Singer."

Jane was a worrier, and she had cause for concern in case of injury or sickness. One time William cut his thumb off in a boating accident, and he had to be taken into Fairbanks for surgery. She was the victim in another accident.

"Dad was away on a trip," Hal said. "There was a trap door in the floor of the trading post that led to the root cellar. One day Mother sent my sisters and me to get vegetables. We did, but neglected to close the trap door. That night when Mother went into the store, with only a candle for light, she fell head-first into the root cellar. Miraculously, she did not break her neck, nor any big bones, but her face was so badly smashed she was almost unrecognizable for weeks."

Another job that fell to Jane was that of teaching the children when they came of school age. Her background as a teacher was valuable.

"Our textbooks were sent from England," Hal said. "Our schooling took place during the winter months and was not rigidly scheduled, but Mother knew how to conduct lessons and compel us to do assigned work.

"We were eager to learn, and did not mind practicing our reading, writing, spelling, and mathematics even during the summer. We received books by Dickens and Doyle from Mother's family over the ocean. There was no trashy reading material in our home. Both our parents spoke correct, slang-free English. A good deal about word usage and sentence structure we learned by example, rather than by grammar rules."

In the Newtons' large garden, watered by buckets of river water, Jane grew the vegetables needed through the winter. She planted sweet peas on the east side of the cabin to receive the early sun. There were beds of California poppies, sweet alyssum, baby breath and nasturtiums.

By the time the children were school age, Jane was in her forties. Her dream of returning to England having done well in a frontier land was still just a dream.

Growing Up

As children at an isolated trading post on the Tanana River, Madge, Kay and Hal Newton romped and roamed the boundless land where there were few signs of habitation between them and the faraway Alaska Range.

The Indians of Healy Lake, five miles upstream, lived in white-walled tents heated with Yukon stoves and lighted with candles. William stocked the tents, stoves, candles and kerosene wick lamps, as well as mantle gasoline lamps at the trading post.

One of the Indians was called "Little White Man" because he had white hair and whiskers. He made beautiful birchbark canoes, and snowshoes.

"They [the snowshoes] were not at all like the French-Canadian or bear paw variety," Hal recalled. "They were less rugged, but lighter, and gave better support in the soft, deep snow. They were made with birch frames and fine rawhide webbing — quite long, with rounded, turned up fronts and tapered, pointed backs. Little White Man also made bows and arrows for my sisters and me, although we never developed any archery skills."

For several years the steamboat *Reliance* made one trip in midsummer to the trading post. Later an Irishman, Captain

Flanigan, made the trip in a smaller steamboat.

"Captain Flanigan was a pleasant and entertaining fellow, and his arrival was the most exciting event of the season," Hal recalled. "Although my sisters and I were bashful, we were thrilled when the steamboat pulled to shore. Here was our chance to get news and a little attention.

"I don't believe I ever felt lonely. My sisters and I were very close, and we had known no other companionship. That was the way things were and had always been."

As Madge, Hal and Kay grew older, Jane taught them to bake cookies, make candy, and do basic sewing. They hiked the wooded hills, hunted grouse and rabbits, and picked wild berries. In the winter they tended a small trap line. There was always water to carry — in the winter they chopped a hole through the river ice — sawing, splitting, and carrying wood for the house, the store and the shed where the goats and chickens were kept.

William had the idea that it would be worthwhile to raise goats and chickens for the eggs and milk they would provide, but mainly they provided more work. Hal said, "During the goat era — which my sisters and I hated — we always ran out of hay before winter's end. That meant we had to take the small team of dogs and harvest endless loads of willow saplings to feed the goats until they could graze."

The Newtons' big garden, a mainstay for the family, was a never-ending job of tilling, weeding and watering, but produced an abundance of radishes, lettuce, peas, onions, carrots, turnips, cabbage, cauliflower and potatoes. The wild berries — red and black currants, raspberries, blueberries and lingonberries — were harvested too.

William fished for pickerel and whitefish, some of which he smoked and salted for winter use, and lingcod for the dogs. Wild game was plentiful. The Newton table offered moose, caribou, beaver, bear, muskrat and rabbit meat. Jane rendered the bear fat to use for butter. Ducks, geese, a few swans and three varieties of grouse and ptarmigan were part of the family fare.

The Tanana River, cold, swift and muddy, was unsuitable for swimming, but William wanted his children to learn that skill.

"One summer day we walked four miles to Hidden Lake," Hal said, "and Dad taught us the basic swimming strokes. All of us became reasonably proficient and unafraid of the water, except Mother. A few times each summer we went camping by poling boat, or motorboat, to the nearby lakes.

"Dad bought a flat-bottomed boat with a single-cylinder marine gasoline engine. In the fall he took the engine off the boat and connected it to a large circular saw to cut logs to stove length. Happily for me, it eliminated hand-sawing firewood.

"I was fascinated by the breakup in the spring. Often the ice was jammed downstream, causing the water level to rise several feet. When the jam finally broke and the water level receded, huge slabs of ice were stranded on the shore and it took days for them to melt. I loved watching the spring and fall flights of the migratory birds. It was most impressive in the fall when the numbers were increased by a new generation. A dozen or more flocks would be in sight all day long as swans, geese, ducks and sandhill cranes flew south."

A Kind of Genius

William Newton had to develop many skills to be self-sufficient at his wilderness post. Hal watched with amazement as his father transformed a used mining boiler into a small sawmill that could cut lumber without whipsawing — a nasty task.

All the goods for the trading post — the canned food, the tools, the steel traps, guns, tents, kerosene, and lamps — had to be freighted in by water or overland, both long and costly routes. For river freighting Newton built a poling boat — a long, narrow, flat-bottomed boat pointed at both bow and stern and equipped with two pike poles and a pair of oars. The nearest supply point was a small settlement with a roadhouse and ferry crossing named McCarty (not to be confused with McCarthy in the Kennicott country) on the Tanana River watershed.

"Floating down the river to McCarty took five easy hours or so," Hal recalled, "but going back up the river was a different story. The current of the Tanana was much too swift for rowing, so two men had to pole and line the boats up the river — a very winding river it was, too. In some places the riverbank was eroded, leaving sweepers (fallen trees) hanging out over the water. The sweepers could knock a man out of his boat if he didn't look out.

"On the inside curves — equally dangerous — were sloughs, sand and gravel bars and drift piles. My Dad and his partner would both be poling with all their stength, or one man would pole while the other went ashore and pulled the boat with the rope.

"Eventually we would pass the bad spot and the boat would

have to be rowed to the opposite side of the river, losing as little headway as possible. This trip upstream took, at best, three days of grueling work. There were times when boat and cargo were lost in the tricky waters of the Tanana."

William, who made long trips by dogsled, designed a sled to better serve his purpose. Conventional dogsleds have runners well below the floor of the basket, and are hard to pull through deep, soft snow. Toboggans are better for that purpose, but they have no handlebars. Newton came up with a practical combination. His dogsled had a toboggan floor and runners, which allowed it to ride like a sleigh in packed snow, and like a toboggan in loose snow. Attached was a conventional sled superstructure with handlebars.

Newton did not operate a trap line, but he did set his massive bear traps each year. The black bears he got each summer augmented the food supply for the dogs and the wild foxes he bred for fur — another venture which was more work than it was worth. Although the trading post was not in the path of the major migration of caribou, herds of forty or fifty animals passed nearby en route to the tundra flats, where they calved and spent the summer. In the fall they returned by the same route on their way to winter grounds near the Alaska Range.

"A full-antlered caribou on the run is a beautiful and awesome sight," Hal said. "When I was eight Dad gave me a rifle. The following year I shot my first caribou. It seems odd to me now, but at that young age my two sisters and I were adept at skinning and butchering wild game."

The Indians at Healy Lake supplied Newton with the mink, beaver, muskrat and fox pelts he sold at the London fur auction. In 1914 his furs were sent out shortly after the outbreak of World War I. Prices suddenly plummeted, and William lost so much money he was bankrupt. It was a cruel blow. William, stubborn and independent, tried to fight his way out of his financial troubles by hanging onto the trading post.

"There were several factors that made this a poor gamble," Hal said. "Fur prices remained poor all through the war years, and fur-bearing animals were becoming more scarce. Tuberculosis and syphilis, introduced by the early prospectors and traders, were taking their toll, and the Indian population was declining. On top of that, two other people went into the trading business near us, competing for the limited business. As a result, the remaining years at the trading post were harsh and lean."

Home in Fairbanks

T he rigors of rearing three children in the wilderness, schooling them, and operating the trading post when her husband was gone, took their toll on Jane. In 1924 she was fifty-one. The children — Madge, fourteen, and the twins Hal and Kay, twelve — had lived their entire life at the trading post. William realized he could no longer deny them a formal education.

They left behind the cabins, the caches, and the chicken house, the goat pen, the fox run, the sawmill and the dog houses. They took with them their homemade clothes, their Indian moccasins and their British accents. They traveled by boat to the McCarty trading post, where they waited for the stage to Fairbanks.

"We had our tents, and we made beds of spruce boughs," Kay Newton Shafer recalled, "but I could not sleep, the hum of the telegraph wires was so loud. We'd been used to complete stillness. The next day Roy Lund's touring car came lumbering down the road. We climbed in and began our all-day journey to town.

"We stopped at Richardson Roadhouse for dinner and ate a fabulous concoction called lemon pie. When we entered the cabin Dad bought in Fairbanks, we discovered the most amazing thing — electric lights. There were light bulbs hanging from the ceiling, and we marveled at such brightness after growing up with candles and kerosene lamps."

Hal recalled, "We lived very frugally in Fairbanks. Even though our house was more adequate than it had been at the trading post, it was minimal by most standards. We had two bedrooms, piped-in water, and an outhouse. Our cabin was heated by a wood stove in the living room where I slept."

The Newtons lived on the same block as the Mary Lee Davis house. At that time it was occupied by the Egleston family; he was with the Fairbanks Exploration Company. Next to their house was a tennis court, which by then was falling apart. "We used it for bicycling and roller skating until it completely collapsed," Hal said. Nearby was the frame cottage where Cleora and George Bachner lived. On occasion Hal sat the Bachners' children.

"When we moved to Fairbanks we were shy and introverted," Hal said. "Our clothing and accent made us a curiosity. We were teased and occasionally ridiculed, and, of course, we were very sensitive. Fortunately, our teachers were understanding, and thanks to our Mother's early tutoring, we had a good educational background.

By the time we were in high school we had developed friendships that lasted long after we left the country."

Kay said, "School wasn't bad except for arithmetic. We had been doing our sums in pounds, shillings and pence, and as a result I got an F in arithmetic the first month. I went about with my nose in the air, and my queer shoes, and homemade clothes, and what others thought about me didn't bother me. What did bother me was that I was overweight, and I couldn't sing a note. I filled space in the Episcopal choir and was smart enough not to make a sound."

During the first two years the Newtons lived in town, William continued to run the trading post. In 1926 he sold the business and went into real estate in Fairbanks. He bought old houses, repaired them, and sold them at a profit. At that time William became a U.S. citizen, but not Jane. She still had her dream.

In 1930, after living in Alaska twenty-two years without a trip Outside, Jane went back to England. While she was gone, William bought a house in Seattle.

"I think Mother found England much changed — not the place she remembered," Hal said. "She must have laid to rest her dream to go back there to live, because shortly after her arrival in Seattle she became a citizen of the United States."

William, who had turned his back on a medical education in England, insisted that his three children attend college. They were enrolled at the University of Washington in 1930.

"Dad kept the family going on a very marginal basis by investing his limited funds — for the most part shrewdly — in the stock market," said Hal. In 1934 all three Newtons graduated — Hal in engineering, Kay in nursing, and Madge in home economics.

William eventually achieved a modest financial security that sustained him and Jane the rest of their lives. He died at eighty-six, in Seattle. Jane lived on alone in a small apartment and died just before her ninety-ninth birthday. Madge died in 1975.

The Newton homestead on the Tanana was sold in 1926 to Emil Hammer, a prospector and trader. When Hammer died, Ted Lowell discovered that neither Newton nor Hammer ever owned the property. He filed on five acres and received title from the federal government. In 1979 Lowell sold the property to Ron and Barbara Short of Fairbanks. Ron was born and reared in England, and his sister lives in Newcastle-on-Tyne where William Newton was born. Not long ago the Shorts visited Ron's sister at her seaside cottage in Newton — a village named in honor of William's surgeon father.

ABOUT THE AUTHOR

Jo Anne Wold was a journalist, historian and author. She hosted a weekly radio show at age sixteen, worked on both Fairbanks newspapers and as a stringer for *Time* magazine, wrote articles for other publications, won thirteen state and national journalism awards, received an honorary doctorate from the University of Alaska. *The Way It Was* is her fifth published book.

Few people outside of Fairbanks, where Jo Anne lived all her short life, knew she was paralyzed from the neck down, had been since she contracted polio at age twelve. "I want to be known for my work," she said, "not for my handicap."

She learned to use a manual typewriter with a pencil between her teeth, finished elementary school, graduated from Lathrop High School, took courses in journalism and creative writing at the University of Alaska. She had a special telephone she could dial and, according to Editor Tom Snapp of *Jessen's Daily*, "a golden voice that oozed enthusiasm. She interviewed over the telephone with more ease than most reporters do in person . . . She was the best reporter on the staff . . . She often scooped other reporters. She even covered a Big Delta buffalo hunt in her wheelchair."

As remarkable as her professional success was her indomitable attitude. She was a happy child in a happy household, and that did not change with adversity. Her widowed mother, two sisters and, eventually, her stepfather, Glen Buchanan, were optimistic and supportive.* As one lifelong friend put it, "Their house radiated with love and cheer." Said another, "Jo Anne was loving and giving, fun to be with, always willing to help those around her."

The happiest day of her life came in September, 1979, when, in white gown and veil, surrounded by family and friends in a flower-festooned church, she and Lee Schroer were married. Together, in a specially equipped van, they explored the Fairbanks area and even traveled to the Lower 48.

This book is Jo Anne's last. She died of pneumonia at age forty-seven.

---

*Jo Anne's mother, Eleanor, died in 1969 of leukemia, the illness that had taken her father, Arnold Wold, in 1948. Lee Schroer is a lineman for the City of Fairbanks. Glenn Buchanan now lives in Anchorage. Jo Anne's older sister, Kay Effenbech, lives in Soldotna, and the youngest, Bonnie Kuykendall, in Florida.

Another absorbing book by Jo Anne Wold

THIS OLD HOUSE

The story of Fairbanks from mining camp to modern city, as seen through the eyes of an intrepid pioneer wife and mother. Clara Hickman was eighteen in 1908, when she came to the North "just for a year." That year stretched to seventy. Clara married Jess Rust, mined with him on the Little Eldorado, converted a log cabin into a spacious and gracious home, reared six children, kept a careful journal and during her last ten years wrote a column for the *Fairbanks Daily News-Miner*.

Jo Anne Wold, one of Clara Rust's countless friends, distilled the story of Clara's life, her home and her city from the journals, the columns and hours of informal interviews.

This Old House is available from Alaska Northwest Publishing Company for $6.95.

M any other fascinating books are available from Alaska Northwest Publishing Company. For a catalog, send your name and address to:

Alaska Northwest Publishing Company

130 Second Avenue South
Edmonds, Washington 98020

or call toll-free 1-800-533-7381